T0291394

Unlocking Sustained Innovation Success in Healthcare

Dr. Greg McLaughlin
Dr. Suzanne Richins

CRC Press
Taylor & Francis Group
Boca Raton London New York

CRC Press is an imprint of the
Taylor & Francis Group, an **informa** business

A PRODUCTIVITY PRESS BOOK

CRC Press
Taylor & Francis Group
6000 Broken Sound Parkway NW, Suite 300
Boca Raton, FL 33487-2742

© 2015 by Taylor & Francis Group, LLC
CRC Press is an imprint of Taylor & Francis Group, an Informa business

No claim to original U.S. Government works

Printed on acid-free paper
Version Date: 20140825

International Standard Book Number-13: 978-1-4822-3980-5 (Hardback)

Library of Congress Cataloging-in-Publication Data

McLaughlin, Gregory C., author.
  Unlocking sustained innovation success in healthcare / Greg McLaughlin, Suzanne Richins.
    p. ; cm.
  Includes bibliographical references and index.
  ISBN 978-1-4822-3980-5 (hardcover : alk. paper)
  I. Richins, Suzanne, author. II. Title.
  [DNLM: 1. Health Care Sector--organization & administration. 2. Delivery of Health Care--organization & administration. 3. Organizational Innovation. W 74.1]

RA418
362.1--dc23
2014033168

Visit the Taylor & Francis Web site at
http://www.taylorandfrancis.com

and the CRC Press Web site at
http://www.crcpress.com

Contents

List of Figures

List of Tables

Preface

This is the first in a series of books on how ENOVALE™ innovation process management operates for a specific market group. Our intent is to demonstrate how the technology is used and how it will provide for innovation success in our first sector, that of healthcare. Innovation is a necessity for healthcare businesses due to the rapidly changing technology in which that business functions. Yet, most innovations come from technical or engineering departments with responsibility for research and development. This selectively misses the dramatic innovations made by individuals both inside and outside the company. In truth, innovations come from human needs that remain unsatisfied. Individuals are best at identifying these needs.

Our research, conducted through the Project Impact Institute, demonstrated that individuals are the life cycle of innovation. Innovation begins and ends with the individual. Given the importance of individuals, the authors designed an innovation process management technology that will enable innovation to flow upward in the organization from individuals. Our research further substantiated that innovation varies from culture to culture, specifically with age, gender, and educational level. To extend our research to the healthcare sector, we surveyed more than 100 nurse executives to obtain their perceptions of innovation and where they see innovation benefiting the organization. The results of this research verify existing results that strongly state that innovation operates in three unique dimensions: (1) new and original innovations, (2) innovations achieved through improvement; and (3) innovations resulting in positive change or replacement.

Numerous examples in this book help demonstrate the principles and practices associated with the ENOVALE process. The ENOVALE process is a combination of both practical innovation management techniques and thorough scholarly research. We included examples of numerous healthcare businesses and practices. In addition, this book has extensively cited authors in the field who add value and justification for the practices developed in the book.

Because of the changing environment in the healthcare sector, a chapter on looking to the future is provided (see Chapter 8). A chapter on leadership in the healthcare sector also provides a unique opportunity to see how methodology will provide for sustained success (see Chapter 9). Finally, a chapter on innovation and the individual closes out the book and stresses how companies, organizations, and nonprofits will benefit from this approach (see Chapter 10).

About the Authors

Dr. Greg McLaughlin possesses a unique talent for taking strategic visions and ideas, and turning them into operational realities. He creates value in organizations through his ability to solve complex problems; recognize hidden or unexplained data patterns; and by creating practical, ready-to-implement solutions. Over the past 30 years, he has developed a passion for innovation excellence resulting in the creation of the ENOVALE™ process. His colleagues refer to him as a 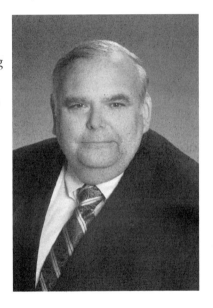 "Renaissance Man," given his diverse sets of life and work experiences that include innovator, hurricane forecaster, author, Six Sigma/Lean "guru," published songwriter, and deacon.

Dr. McLaughlin's diverse background includes extensive time working with management/project methodologies for innovation success. He created the first set of comprehensive Black Belt materials for the Six Sigma Academy, where he was credited with over $300 million of cost savings over a 5-year period. In addition to his Senior Master Black Belt status, he honed his skills as a quality management consultant working directly for Dr. W. Edwards Deming.

Dr. McLaughlin has held two executive positions in the manufacturing, medical products, security, and process industries. He was the CEO of Inthesis, Inc., a successful business intelligence company, and is currently senior vice president for research and development at Global Targeting, Inc., an international strategy and advising firm dedicated to sustained innovation success.

Publication credits include numerous academic and practitioner journal articles, and author of *Total Quality in Research & Development* (1995), and the primary author of *Chance or Choice: Unlocking Innovation Success* (2013), *ENOVALE™: How to Unlock Sustained Innovation Project Success* (2013), *Leading Latino Talent to Champion Innovation* (2013), and *Unlocking Sustained Innovation Success in Healthcare* (2014).

His educational achievements include a doctorate in business administration from Nova Southeastern University, and a master of science degree in statistics and an undergraduate degree in meteorology from the Florida State University. Greg was the director of doctoral research at Nova Southeastern University and presently holds a core faculty position at Capella University.

Dr. Suzanne Richins is known as an early adopter of technology and innovation. As a senior leader in healthcare, she was one of the first to look at using analytics to structure staffing schedules based on patient arrival acuity to the Emergency Department for her masters' thesis. The methodology was adopted throughout Intermountain  Healthcare and various other well-known healthcare systems. While serving on the American Hospital Association

Board and The Joint Commission Advisory Committee, she conducted her dissertation on patient satisfaction prior to the adoption of these standards by both of these respected organizations. Her latest work is in using analytics to predict patient outcomes and improve quality. She also teaches doctor of business administration (DBA), doctorate in healthcare administration (DHA), and doctorate in nursing practice (DNP) students for various universities.

Dr. Richins earned her nursing degree from Weber State University, her professional arts degree from St. Joseph's College, her MBA from Utah State University, and her doctorate in healthcare administration at the Medical University of South Carolina. She earned her degrees while advancing from staff nurse to manager of the operating rooms, director of Emergency and Urgent Care Clinics, director of Medical/Surgical Services, administrator of Freestanding Surgical Centers, and Chief Operating Officer.

Due to her varied education and experience, Dr. Richins currently provides consultation and advising to clients about software for electronic medical records, revenue cycle management, and predictive and retrospective analytics. She is the senior vice president for healthcare at Global Targeting, Inc.

Chapter 1

Introduction

Background

When people think about innovation in healthcare, they think of miracle drugs; new technology; minimally invasive surgeries and procedures; new equipment for monitoring patients' vital signs, heart rhythms, and function; robotic surgery; and remote monitoring. Essentially, all the aforementioned innovations are, in fact, inventions or discoveries. These advancements improved the delivery of care, making it possible for outpatient procedures and home care, thus allowing patients to remain at home instead of in a hospitalized environment. These inventions and discoveries comprise events that save lives and improve society. Events, however, occur sporadically with no predictability. Inventions and discoveries are unplanned and, as such, offer little advantage when it comes to sustained success. Innovation is more than an event; it also occurs on a daily basis with planning and often with little or no fanfare. Innovation is more than invention; it is both improvement and change. However, now the healthcare industry, like most other industries, needs to focus on innovation as a means to create value, reduce costs, and increase the quality of the care delivered. The margins are smaller than ever and may continue to decline with the implementation of Obamacare. Over the past 30 years, healthcare leaders moved from quality assurance to quality improvement and are now using more sophisticated techniques, such as predictive analytics, to streamline processes, products, and services. A variety of other incentives and methodologies also were used as catalysts for reformation. To understand the present need for innovation, one needs to understand efforts from the past.

The healthcare sector is a broad set of businesses and organizations consisting of biotech, medical products, pharmaceutical, diagnostics, long-term healthcare, hospitals, and home healthcare (Industry Browser, Yahoo finance, 2014). Innovation exists and flourishes in the form of new technology, products, and services. This sector ranges from manufacturing to services with the objective of serving the health and wellness needs of individuals. At present, the healthcare sector accounts for over 18% of the GDP (Gross Domestic Product) (17.9% in 2011) with it rising to 20% by 2021 (Wayne, 2012). Innovation will be critical for this industry to cut costs while providing a quality experience to patients. Given its importance to the economy, this sector will be closely watched to see how innovation is implemented and whether it can sustain success over time.

This book contains an examination of how a broader understanding of innovation in healthcare will unlock sustained success. Numerous examples will amplify how and what innovation is and why it is more than pure invention or discovery. It will include a strategy for creating an effective innovation process management and project success. In addition, concepts such as leadership, the future of innovation, and the importance of the individual to innovation success are presented. Before addressing these concepts, the book begins by describing how the importance of innovation has grown and how its mission has expanded in the healthcare sector.

Innovation is truly the "mother of necessity" because it begins with an unsatisfied need. These needs took humanity from hunter-gatherers to technological marvels. The process was quite erratic (and at times painfully slow) until the twentieth century and the advent of electrical power. Cheap and reliable energy changed society by increasing a million-fold the need for various products, technologies, and services. Healthcare was one of the great recipients of innovation. The results increased longevity, improved the quality of life, eradicated diseases, and reduced pain and suffering. Innovation, in healthcare, is associated with discoveries and technological inventions. Over the past 40 or so years, the emphasis was on quality (products, services, delivery to the patient). Innovation shares many of the same goals and objectives of continuous quality improvement, and the need for innovation merged with this quality perspective.

Historically, healthcare was late in venturing into the quality improvement cycle used by other industries. Other industries followed the research and theories, and adopted the methodology of W. Edwards Deming and Joseph Juran. However, physicians were very reluctant to adopt these principles, stating that patients were not machines or processes, and that the unique make-up of the human being precluded the use of what they termed "cookbook medicine." To avoid the perception of "cookbook medicine," the term "evidence-based medicine" was created. A Medline (HHS, 2002) search shows that the emergence of the term "evidence-based medicine" started in 1995 and escalated to nearly 3,000 references in the literature by 2002 (Claridge and Fabian, 2005).

Quality Assurance and Quality Improvement

As other industries focused on quality, they adopted quality circles and quality improvement techniques. In the 1980s, The Joint Commission for Healthcare Organizations (TJC) added quality assurance to the accreditation requirements. This initial focus required auditing care to ensure that physicians and employees in organizations followed the policies and procedures adopted by the boards of these organizations. In malpractice cases, the first test was whether the caregivers in the organization followed its (the organization's) own policies and procedures. Attorneys typically reviewed the organization's policies and procedures, and compared them to those used in the community to establish a standard of care. The comparison was used as evidence in alleged malpractice suits. The community standard usage meant that all care was local. There was no national standard.

In contrast, pharmaceutical, biotech, and medical products companies eagerly pursued quality improvement techniques and invested heavily in continuous improvement training. Improvements came from projects that addressed a specific problem. However, most organizations never saw the benefits these programs promised. One of the key reasons was that financial systems did not track costs or benefits on a per-project basis. Intrinsic benefits to the organization included an increased awareness of quality assurance, employee involvement, and patient satisfaction. Within a few years, however, interest diminished and organizations either reduced support or redirected their efforts.

The healthcare sector provides a tremendous amount of experience with innovation, with the majority classified as new products, new pharmaceutical discoveries, or new technological applications. These innovations generally originated in the Research and Development (R&D) or Engineering functions. These functions created innovation in the form of new products, technologies, and discoveries that are critical for the survival of the organization. For these businesses, innovation relates directly to competitive advantage. Yet, innovation outside these functions is uncommon, as it is in most technical companies. This history provides an opportunity for innovation to expand outside the expected norm.

For nontechnical healthcare businesses and organizations, innovation usage focused on ways to decrease costs, improve efficiencies, and offer more value to patients and employees alike. This paradigm creates a struggle for some because innovation must be defined differently than inventions or new discoveries. This book will provide a strategy for these organizations as well as those functions that operate outside the traditional innovation generators.

Intermountain Healthcare led the industry in developing research for best clinical practices by introducing a culture based on Quality, Utilization, and Efficiency (QUE) in 1986. Then in 1990, leadership implemented the research institute. At that time, they required all managers, directors, and senior executives to attend training on total quality management. As part of the training, each participant was required to conduct an improvement project. The projects are available for review on their website (Intermountain, n.d.). They expanded the training to people outside the Intermountain network.

Based on these individual projects, Intermountain Healthcare Research Institute's leadership decided to share information across its healthcare system. One of their first organization-wide studies involved the differences in cost and quality of total hip replacement surgery. The study first required that all patients scheduled for total hip surgery in their twenty-three hospitals fill out the SF-36® Health Survey to determine age, mobility, and mental acuity. After surgery at 3-month intervals, the patients filled out the same survey. The outcome of the surgery depended on the initial results of the SF-36 and the type of implant used. The patient's self-assessment scores determined an increase or decrease in the scores derived from surgery. The results showed that orthopedic surgeons did not take into account the age, mobility, or mental acuity of the patient when selecting a prosthesis. Most used the same implant on every patient, regardless of their health status. Once the study was shared with the orthopedic surgeons, a program of demand matching was implemented. The age, mental acuity, and mobility of the patient were incorporated into the selection of the appropriate implant. It was one of their first studies related to the appropriateness of care for the individual patient and resulted in cost-specific selection to meet the needs of individual patients. A 90-year-old patient did not require the same type of implant as a 50-year-old patient. The 90-year-old did well with a cemented prosthesis, and the 50-year-old needed a ceramic porous type (latest technology at that time).

In the 1990s, regulators and accrediting agencies changed the focus from adherence to standards, to evaluating the process of care. The new regulations identified process improvement using continuous quality improvement methodologies formulated by quality "gurus" such as W. Edwards Deming. Their methods focused on total quality management. These methodologies integrated leadership principles, team dynamics, and statistical analysis to determine what processes were out-of-control in order to bring them back into compliance. In 1999, the Institute of Medicine (IOM) estimated the number of deaths each year that were related to medical errors. The results were astounding, yet no one could determine an accurate number. They estimated it was somewhere around 100,000 per year. Even with the lack of a specific number, physicians and administrators acknowledged that the basis for the report was accurate. Next, the IOM released a report (Institute of Medicine, 1999) identifying six areas of focus for improving patient care:

1. Delivering safe care free from accidental or unintentional injury
2. Providing effective care using scientifically based treatment regimes and eliminating unnecessary care
3. Including patients in decisions about their own care and providing them with options and alternatives
4. Eliminating unnecessary wait times to provide care in a timely manner
5. Focusing on efficiency and avoiding waste
6. Ensuring equity through delivery of care separate from the factors of age, gender, race, income, education, or location

These areas were targeted for improvement using evidence-based medicine, meaning that care was delivered based on the scientific method.

Evidence-Based Medicine Adoption

Evidence-based medicine relies on clinical studies with systematic research, and is peer reviewed. Meta-analysis is a mechanism for reviewing multiple studies on the same topic to identify best practices and results. Collation of evidence comes from multiple studies (often conducted at the same time) instead of from just one clinical trial (Pub-Med, 2012). The use of systematic reviews of treatments and prevention methods was identified by researchers as a means of supporting the selection of best practices and guidelines, which resulted in informed decision making. These reviews actually formed the foundation for evidence-based medicine. Some synonyms for evidence-based medicine include "evidence syntheses," "comparative effectiveness reviews," and "health technology assessments" (Pub-Med, 2013).

Don Berwick, MD was one of the first champions of evidence-based medicine; he published through his nonprofit organization, the Institute for Healthcare Improvement (IHI). He was able to enlist the support of renowned hospitals and physicians for implementation of these evidence-based protocols. In 2004, he initiated a campaign and voluntarily signed up two-thirds of the 5,000 hospitals in the United States for the IHI 100,000 Lives Campaign (Institute for Healthcare Improvement, 2004). There were six goals for this program:

1. Deploy rapid response teams (respond to patients identified for imminent crisis).
2. Prevent adverse drug events (reaction to medications causing untoward effects).

3. Deliver reliable, evidence-based care for acute myocardial infarctions (follow a standard protocol for care).
4. Prevent surgical site infections (adopt techniques that prevent patients from acquiring infections related to surgery).
5. Prevent central line infections (follow procedures proven to eliminate infections in patients with an IV in their main veins).
6. Prevent ventilator-associated infections (pneumonia was a common complication of patients on a ventilator).

The campaign was very successful and the protocols were widely accepted. They became the precursors for computer alerts in electronic medial records. The standard of care was no longer community based, but rather evidence-based medicine, and the community created global standards. The integration of these protocols into the order sets of electronic records (known as computerized physician order entry, CPOE)) changed the autonomy of physicians to place orders from without any restrictions to one requiring them to annotate why they chose not to follow the evidence-based order set. Bates et al. (2003) studied the adoption of evidence-based protocols and decided that the only way to ensure adoption was to include them in the clinical decision support standards in electronic order sets. As a side note, the IHI still encourages the use of quality improvement techniques to improve care. The Patient Protection and Affordable Care Act (PPACA) contains requirements called "meaningful use." One of these requirements was the inclusion of CPOE and the adoption of electronic medical records by 2014.

Checklists

As a model for improving care, leaders in healthcare focused on how the airline industry famously reduced accidents using checklists. During the past decade (2000–2010), the healthcare industry focused on adopting checklists to ensure safety precautions. The Joint Commission adopted the Universal Protocol (2003), a strategy for eliminating surgery on the wrong site, safe communication, and other safety factors.

Atul Gawande (2009), a surgeon, was the first recognized proponent of checklists, which he experienced by using the checklist designed as a universal protocol to ensure surgery occurred on the right person and on the right body part. His interest occurred during the construction of a new wing at the hospital where he worked. Gawande noted that contractors in the building trade used checklists and Gantt charts to track progress and to ensure that all the disciplines worked together in a coordinated effort to meet timelines and goals. Gawande determined that the disciplines in patient care could do the same thing. The idea behind the checklists (he found in the literature and the ones he designed) were used to get the team members talking about the patient and focused on the issues specific to the individual patient. Gawande also learned from the Boeing experts that the checklist (a standard in manufacturing industries) must be simple, easy to understand, and written in the language of the profession, using both upper- and lowercase letters in sans serif or Helvetica script. Gawande was in charge of implementing surgery checklists around the globe for the World Health Organization; they were implemented in 2009. Many organizations, along with the accreditation and regulatory agencies, now require these checklists.

Toyota Principles

Virginia Mason Health System in Seattle added a different tactic. In 2002, they took their senior leaders to Japan to see the Toyota Principles in action and decided to use the Toyota strategy to minimize waste and improve quality. They termed their program, Toyota Production System. Since adopting this methodology, they received recognition from various healthcare entities for their improvements. For example, they reported, "In most hospitals, nurses spend about 35 percent of their time in direct patient care. With the implementation of VMPS, Virginia Mason Medical Center nursing teams increased it to 90 percent. They used RPIWs [rapid process improvement work] to evaluate their work and make improvements. Instead of caring for patients throughout a unit, nurses work as a team with a patient-care technician in "cells" (groups of rooms located near each other). The cell model allows nurses to monitor patients and quickly attend to needs. Also, the most commonly used supplies for each unit were moved to patient rooms so nurses reduced walking back and forth to get supplies. Steps walked per day fell from 10,000 to roughly 1,200." (Virginia Mason, n.d.).

Six Sigma

Six Sigma was developed at Motorola and came into prominence under the guidance of Jack Welch at GE, who wanted to institute quality improvement as a standard practice. The prime purpose of Six Sigma is to create and sustain processes that produce nearly defect-free products and services. Operational and process problems are identified and improved using the Six Sigma strategy. Six Sigma uses a simple strategy consisting of Define, Measure, Analyze, Improve, and Control (DMAIC). Six Sigma achieves success by improving a process that meets customer (patient) requirements. Many organizations provide Six Sigma training, wherein participants earn belts (levels of sophistication) as they move through the techniques and competencies from green belt to black belt. Six Sigma includes the use of cause-and-effect analysis, statistical analysis, and stringent control plans. Six Sigma training and certification were very popular in the healthcare research and manufacturing businesses. Elements of this methodology continue today.

During the 1990s and early 2000s, Six Sigma training and leadership techniques were also quite popular in health-care facilities. Many major hospital conglomerates, such as Health Corporation of America (HCA), invested heavily in Six Sigma training. Even regional and local hospital organizations invested in Six Sigma, designating an executive to manage this process. Success was often spotty, especially in areas such as the Human Resources, Finance, and Legal departments, where process identification is not a regular procedure. However, to this day, a Six Sigma Black Belt or Master Black Belt certification is required for many quality- or engineering-related jobs.

Lean Techniques

Industrial engineers lead projects to drive out waste in supplies, equipment, and personnel while providing care. The idea is to maximize capacity while increasing quality and decreasing costs. Lean training includes five principles: Sort, Straighten, Sweep, Standardize, and Sustain. The 5S provide a foundation for cleaning, organizing, creating policies and procedures, and ensuring they continue. A good example of Lean process improvement comes from an operating room study at Parkridge Hospital on turnover times. Using these Lean techniques, they were able to reduce turnover times by 45%, meaning they could conduct more surgeries every day in the same amount of time without increasing labor costs while increasing utilization (Marshall et al., 2006).

Comparative Effectiveness Research

When President Obama appointed Don Berwick, MD, to head the Centers for Medicare & Medicaid Services (CMS), Berwick initiated the same techniques he espoused during his tenure at the Institute for Healthcare Improvement. He encouraged quality improvement, standardized order sets that were hard-wired into electronic health records orders, and initiated pay-for-performance and comparative effectiveness research (CER) as part of the PPACA of 2010 (also known as Obamacare). Of note, CER was also included in two previous legislative acts, the American Recovery and Reinvestment Act of 2009 and the Health Information Technology for Economic and Clinical Health (HITECH) Act of 2009. Inclusion of CER in these laws was to ensure that research supported clinical guidelines.

FMEA and Root Cause Analysis

Two other methodologies were adopted to analyze the outcome of errors and near-miss adventures and malpractice to identify not only what happened, but also to determine why it happened, and to prevent any future occurrences. These methodologies are failure modes and effectiveness analysis (FMEA) and root cause analysis. Both were adopted by industry as quality improvement methodologies. Root cause analysis retrospectively looks at what happened to cause an unexpected event. The methodology includes asking "why" five times in order to find the root cause. In contrast, FEMA is prospective analysis that concentrates on prevention instead of identification of cause.

The Joint Commission expects organizations to use these tools as part of their risk management activities. They are listed in their standards and their tool kit (The Joint Commission, n.d.). For example, Good Samaritan Hospital in Chicago (Adachi and Lodolce, 2005) used FMEA to identify potential problems with IV drug administration and was able to design a process that eliminated many potential errors. Stewart et al. (2011) used root cause analysis to reduce surgical site infections. Healthcare leaders use these tools as ways to reduce costs by preventing errors, as errors give rise costly care to treat the consequences of the error. Insurance companies and government payors no longer reimburse organizations for errors and subsequent costly treatments. These events are now termed "never-events" (avoidable complications).

These never-events are not specific to the United States. They were adopted in several countries where the events are also not reimbursed. Harrop-Griffiths (2011) described how the National Healthcare System in the United Kingdom used these never-events to redesign care delivery in an effort to eliminate them by creating a safety culture. The shift from blame identification to safety also occurred in the United States.

In 2011, The National Quality forum (AHRQ, Patient Safety Net, n.d.) listed twenty-nine never-events, emphasizing that these kinds of incidents are avoidable, costly, and often create long-term problems for patients. The focus on these events creates an opportunity for prevention, which improves the quality of care. These events often prolong hospitalization. The AHRQ site includes a discussion of the twenty-nine different types of incidents, and contains primers on how to avoid the events in the first place. The primers are a good place to start on prevention; however, innovation may alter the processes and eliminate the cause of these events.

Employers also expressed concern over never-events. They formed an organization called the Leapfrog Group that collects data about quality providers. They also developed a calculator for use by employers to see how never-events add costs that the employer pays (Hidden Surcharge Calculator, 2013).

Pay-for-Performance

Pay-for-performance (P4P) incentivizes physicians to improve the health of the patients they serve. Instead of paying for visits and treatments, the program emphasizes the improvement of the individual patient's health status by treating chronic diseases and maintaining an optimal state of physical and mental activity. Ideally, providers also treat chronic and infectious diseases through prevention and early identification. A demonstration project was also included in the PPACA. Yet, Houle et al. (2012) found that it only marginally improved care and outcomes. The authors conducted a meta-analysis of thirty studies to determine the effect on clinical outcomes and mortality. As with other reimbursement models, there was little effect on patient outcome or processes. The research continues because, intuitively, it makes sense.

The Evolution to Innovation

Quality improvement efforts are operational by intent. Organizations implemented projects to demonstrate the usefulness of these practices and, when feasible, incorporated the practices into daily routines; improvements are incremental with the goal of financial benefit and process improvement. As healthcare professionals sought to improve both the bottom line and patient satisfaction, it was obvious that some improvements needed to be more than incremental. These improvements needed to leap-frog similar competitive organizations. The primary rationale focused on innovation to change the marketplace, redefine a "new normal," or find a reason to change.

Innovation emerged as a topic in many boardrooms among leaders and administrators alike. Leaders want to know how to strategically move the organization toward an innovative culture focused on more than new discoveries or inventions, but also focusing on everyday practices. Innovation befits the organization from a lower cost perspective to improved communications, a responsive and motivated workforce, and working within cultural and ethnic diversity. In essence, innovation was released by the Research and Development function to operations within each department or functional unit in the organization. Outside influences (lower reimbursements, brand dominance, competitive pressures) drive innovation efforts.

Government-Sponsored Innovation

The Centers for Medicare & Medicaid Services also promote demonstration projects that are designated experiments designed to reduce costs and increase quality. "The Centers for Medicare & Medicaid Services (CMS) conducts and sponsors a number of innovative demonstration projects to test and measure the effect of potential program changes. Our demonstrations study the likely impact of new methods of service delivery, coverage of new types of service, and new payment approaches on beneficiaries, providers, health plans, states, and the Medicare Trust Funds. Evaluation projects validate our research and demonstration findings and help us monitor the effectiveness of Medicare, Medicaid, and the Children's Health Insurance Program (CHIP)." The reports of these projects are found on the government website with the idea that reading the reports may spur even more innovation by providers (Medicare Demonstration Projects, n.d.). They range from how care is delivered in various settings to transitions of care from setting-to-setting, along with coordination of different processes within departments.

Both the PPACA and Section 1115A of the Social Security Act required the CMS to support innovation for new payment methods and delivery of care (Innovation Center, n.d.). The CMS website contains forty-one different innovations currently in progress. The aging of the population, the costs of technology, and the increase in morbid conditions in the population highlighted the need to reimburse providers for innovating delivery models and payment structures.

Professional Societies and Associations

Highly respected organizations, such as the American Medical Association (AMA), sponsor programs on innovation in medicine. The American Organization for Nursing Executives (AONE) sponsored an innovation survey to determine how members perceive innovation. The results of that survey are included in this book. The American Hospital Association (AHA) possesses its own "Centers of Innovation." The Center for Healthcare Innovation held its 2nd Annual Summit in May of 2014. These professional societies understand the need for assisting their members with the topic of innovation as it applies to healthcare.

This call to action swelled into a chorus of voices all acclaiming the need for innovation. Of course, some will say this is a "fad"—as was quality improvement, Six Sigma, and Lean. Yet, these programs continue to serve a purpose. In this book, the authors demonstrate how innovation is more than a "fad"; it is achievable results driven by competition.

In 2005, Kaiser Permanente initiated a program to identify patients with diabetes or heart disease in order to prevent strokes. Their evidenced-based intervention contains a simple bundle of low-cost medications that they prescribe with a beta-blocker and an exercise program. They now tout that 65,000 patients in sixty locations receive care based on their quality improvement program (Kaiser, n.d.).

The Cleveland Clinic designed a similar program that improved blood sugar level control by 32%. At the same time, it decreased by 50% the number of patients who missed an appointment. They instituted nurse navigators to help patients stay in compliance with their treatment plans (Pogoric, 2014).

The Need for Innovation

The historical review of quality improvement in healthcare showed that continuous quality improvement provided a mechanism to get teams together to talk about the patient experience and the steps in the care process. Diagramming the process in flowcharts provided a focus on the care rather than blaming those involved in the steps for any problems. It changed the dynamic from isolated processes in silos to coordinated processes. Once the focus changed to coordination, the root cause of many errors was identified as a lack of communication about the care and patient status as patients moved from one care center to another. Quality Improvement became a sound operational strategy, but what was needed was a more dramatic outcome.

Innovation is not about incremental improvement, but rather it is about breakthroughs that change the existing paradigm. Innovation is recognized when expectations are exceeded and needs, wants, or desires are met. Patients need to be more than satisfied; they require a reset in what they have come to expect. Innovations can be everything from a new drug discovery to operating more efficiently than anyone expected. Innovation challenges us to reset what we expect, how it is delivered, and how it performs. A new drug that does not meet expectations or delivers a benefit less than desired is not innovative. Just because it is new does not mean it is innovative!

The SBAR (Situation-Background-Assessment-Recommendation), developed by the Institute for Healthcare Improvement (ihi.org, 2011) was identified as the language for communicating the care provided and the current problem needs of the patient. Medication reconciliation and checklists ensure that no gaps occur in information pertinent to the next stage of care.

These improvements demonstrate the need to move to the next step where the culture in the organization makes it possible for every individual to innovate. Individuals performing the work often possess good ideas on how to improve the process, increase efficiency, improve overall quality, and improve patient satisfaction. They just need permission from management to innovate and a method to follow that has proven successful. The ENOVALE™ process provides the method to implement an innovation project. Management must ensure that a culture exists to support innovation at all levels in the organization.

ENOVALE is a trademarked innovation management process of Global Targeting, Inc. and provides a framework for implementing innovation within any organization or function.

This framework, its initial use across industries, and research in the healthcare industry are presented in this book.

Organization of the Remaining Chapters

This book consists of ten chapters.
- Chapter 2 describes how Global Targeting, Inc. defines the "means" of innovation.
- Chapter 3 describes the results of the AONE (American Organization of Nursing Executives) Survey on Innovation. AONE is a subsidiary of the American Hospital Association.
- Chapter 4 defines innovation for new and original products, technology, and services.
- Chapter 5 explains how innovation can be improvement while meeting a need.
- Chapter 6 uses the idea of change and how innovation affects decision making.
- Chapter 7 discusses the performance metrics so key to innovation.
- Chapter 8 examines the future of innovation in healthcare.
- Chapter 9 explores the interaction of leadership and innovation.
- Chapter 10 reviews why the individual is so critical to innovation.

Summary

This "Introduction" provided an overview of innovation, especially in the healthcare sector. Learning from the past provides knowledge and experience to ensure a better future. Knowledge of the history of healthcare, its foray into quality improvement, and the critical need for innovation in the future provide an excellent backdrop for discussing what elements are needed for future success. Given the importance of this sector and what it adds to the economy, the research provides a picture of what the future holds in terms of society's dependence on innovative practices.

Discussion Questions

1. After examining the history of evolution and focus on healthcare quality from quality assurance to innovation, evaluate how the external forces shape the need for innovation today.
2. In previous decades, leaders focused on the need for teams to work together on quality improvement and to utilize structured techniques for this process. Teams still need to collaborate on improving processes, yet there still exists a need for *individual* innovation. Defend this need.
3. The Patient Protection and Affordable Care Act (PPACA) of 2010 includes innovation centers. Justify why innovation was identified for inclusion in this legislation.

Assignment

Interview two or three people who participated in quality improvement efforts in the past. Tell respondents that you need about 15 minutes of their valuable time. Ask them the following questions (or questions similar to these):

1. What was your overall impression of the activities and its successes?
2. Does management support the effort so that it continues today?
   a. If not, what do you think went wrong?
   b. What correction would you propose?
3. What techniques or tools do you still use?
   a. If none, why not?
   b. What is the impact of not using techniques or tools?

4. Did everyone in the organization "buy in" to the philosophy, training, and application of tools and practices?
   a. If not, why do you think that some felt positively and
   others felt less so?
   b. Explain how this perception could be changed.
5. What is your lasting impression of these efforts?
   a. Did it change the organization?
   b. Did it meet some objective or goal set by management?
   c. Does the organization function better today as a result
   of this effort?

Assemble the responses and look for similarities and differences. Summarize the results, highlighting when respondents
agree and disagree. What learning can you deduce from
these respondents?

Chapter 2

How Innovation
Is Different

Introduction

One common question asked is how innovation differs from
techniques such as Quality Improvement and Six Sigma. These
techniques encourage continuous improvement, improved
efficiencies, and greater productivity—all critical goals for most
organizations. Yet, innovation is different, as the goal of innovation is to take the organization to its next logical develop-
mental step. This chapter answers the question and provides
specific reasons why innovation does not replace continuous
improvement but moves the business or organization forward
toward significant cost savings, sustained competitive advantage, and significant customer (patient) satisfaction.

Improvement Techniques

The mantra for quite some time concentrated on improvement
of quality for the customer (patient), worker, physician, or
administrator. Quality improvement was, historically, a method

to improve both process and product, while increasing customer satisfaction. Authors such as W. Edwards Deming, Joseph Juran, and Mikel Harry, and the Toyota Production System created a sense of urgency with regard to improving quality for continued financial success and organizational performance. Deming was known for his 14 Principles of Leadership, Juran for Quality Practices and Processes, Harry for Six Sigma defect reduction, and Toyota for defect-free production. All four (and many more) contributed to increasing awareness of quality improvement and customer satisfaction. Success came from the manufacturing sector by identifying defects (the results of poor quality) and containing their effects. Over time, awareness of these philosophies extended to other sectors, such as healthcare, resulting in reasonable successes. The one problem was that many organizations had no collective knowledge of what a defect was or how it influenced financial performance. In healthcare, every encounter was considered a unique experience and every patient unique. Standardization of the workflow was not considered until the late 1990s when leadership started paying attention to errors. The Institute of Medicine (IOM, 2001) released a report estimating that 98,000 patients died each year due to medical errors. At the time, the paradigm regarded manufacturing as not fully applicable to other industries such as those concentrated in the service sector. To understand this disconnect, consider the "process" used to identify and correct a defect.

To initiate an improvement project, a problem was identified. The problem was due to a process, operation, or customer defect. A defect is a tangible item that fails to meet requirements. However, in healthcare, these "defects" were considered serendipitous events due to the patient differences. In manufacturing, the philosophy is to identify and prevent the defect from occurring. This philosophy comes from the manufacturing sector as a way to ensure adherence to standards (a definition of quality) while improving efficiencies and reducing waste. It worked so well that the philosophy spread to other industries—to any organization with a defined customer and an identifiable problem caused by a defect.

No one quantified waste in healthcare. The payment system was fee-for-service, meaning that every action had a separate charge code and patients were billed for these charges, including the cost of treating an infection that the patient acquired as part of their treatment. Therefore, no one focused on the need to correct and prevent errors. Under the fee-for-service model, payors reimbursed providers based on a percentage depending upon the terms of the contract. Providers (hospitals and physicians) set their prices based on expected reimbursement. If a patient had an untoward outcome due to an error, the payor still paid for the error using the contracted percentage discount. The government payors used a Diagnostic Related Group (DRG) payment system. If an untoward event occurred, the DRG was upgraded and changed to include this untoward event.

There was no change in this methodology until 2008 when Medicare and Medicaid provided a list of "never-events" and notified providers that no reimbursement would occur for treatment of errors listed in the "never-events" category (CMS, 2007). The commercial payors followed the lead of these government payors. They adopted the same list of "never-events".

Many non-manufacturers had difficulty relating this defect-free philosophy to their operations. Yet for those who tried it, successes occurred in the organizations using these tools and, therefore, the techniques were difficult to dispute. Service businesses do not produce in the same manner as a manufacturer. The difficulty lies in convincing the provider that a "process" exists to initiate the service. Techniques such as Lean Six Sigma helped to establish the concept of a process where inefficiencies can rob profits. However, progress was slow and with time, the effort dissipated.

Healthcare, too, experienced a variety of successes as well as inconclusive results. Early attempts at Total Quality Management were successful in some organizations (medical products, pharmaceuticals, hospitals, healthcare providers) as leadership decided on the importance of quality improvement to the organization. For example, an individual physician or an individual organization might standardize a process to decrease an untoward event (defect), but the knowledge and know-how was not transferred from physician to physician or organization to organization. These early adopters provided a solid roadmap for others, yet with time, the efforts, funding, and interest dissipated. As a sector, however, remnants of these efforts remain.

Manufacturers and service industries scored a number of successes in their individual organizations using these tools and techniques. These organizations invested great amounts of cash, time, and resources in these programs. Some had success but others could not see a defined and sustained benefit with the methodologies presented. The philosophy made sense to many but the reality did not always perform as expected. In fact, many organizations failed to realize the fundamental changes needed to sustain this philosophy. In reality, defects were not due to single-point causes but were intertwined within the fabric of the organization. The fix for one defect often created another one. In addition, accounting systems were unable to track and isolate project benefits. A project could save $250,000 but if spending increased that much due to uncontrolled or unpredictable causes, the net benefits were lost. Without a defined benefit, what was the reason for the improvement? Many organizations decided to end their efforts without fundamentally accepting the tenets of the philosophy. This failure greatly affected the workforce, who perceived management as unresponsive to change or lukewarm to improvement.

Continuous improvement efforts were (are) successful in reducing the number and severity of defects, alleviating a problem and setting new norms for product, process, or service. However, when completed or disengaged, employees tend to revert quickly to old behaviors. Teams dissolve and/or lose cohesiveness. Individuals often feel less empowered, less needed. Not only does the organization lose benefits, but also employees feel less motivated to perform. If employees put work and effort into a change and see the positive effects of the change only to watch abandonment after dissolution of the team, then discouragement and disengagement set in. The aftermath is often an environment not much different than before the process began. The difficulty arises when trying to "fit" a culture of continuous improvement into an organization that is not prepared for this philosophical shift. The same was true in the healthcare sector; it also suffered from the same loss of engagement. Some improvements did occur, and many adopted these practices and developed language and methods to use the quality improvement methods.

Even the healthcare accrediting body, The Joint Commission, initiated criteria for process improvement. They called this project ORYX, its first foray into performance measurement and improvement. The Joint Commission's performance measurement and improvement initiative appeared in 1997. The ORYX program integrated outcomes (patient health status improvement) and other performance measured data (like patient satisfaction) into the accreditation process (The Joint Commission, 2013). The surveyors reviewed these process improvement programs as presented without any concern for sustainability. Leadership presented these outcomes from process improvement teams during accreditation surveys. However, there was no longitudinal tracking from one accrediting survey to the next. If the initiative was abandoned between surveys, there were no repercussions except to the morale of the employees who worked on these process improvement teams.

Processing Conditions

Given the strong influence of manufacturing, these techniques use a strong processing mentality. Process improvement is a hallmark of success with these ideas. Yet, service businesses struggle to think of themselves as a series of process-oriented units. For example, in healthcare, each department acted independently of all other departments in a hospital. (The studies conducted in the lab were not associated with decision making that affected the need for imaging studies.) Each ancillary department processed orders and only the physicians looked for integration of the results from the individual tests. Patient flow was not considered, nor was the timing of tests or results factored into a seamless process. Rather, each event was thought of as unique and special. Defects were associated with mistakes and errors, and efficiencies were comparable to those defined in the manufacturing and process industries. Reports of limited success exist within the broader service sector.

The other problem was the omission of the continuous portion of the process. When the project or team dissolved, no one monitored to ensure that maintenance of the new process adoptions continued. Over time, human behavior reverts to previous habits, new people come on board, and the solution or change is lost. Instead, innovation requires hard-wiring the solution into the process to avoid dependency on the work of an ad-hoc team. The adoption of computerized physician order entry (CPOE) is the first foray for integrating and hard-wiring these solutions.

There are healthcare organizations that have mastered continuous quality improvement (CQI), as evidenced by the reduced payments they receive. With the fee-for-service model, Medicare pays different amounts for post acute care. For example, "In Connecticut, Medicare beneficiaries are more than twice as likely to end up in a nursing home as they are in Arizona. Medicare spends $8,800 on each Louisiana patient getting home health care, $5,000 more than it spends on the average New Jersey senior. In Chicago, one out of four Medicare beneficiaries receives additional services after leaving the hospital—three times the rate in Phoenix (Rau, 2013). These lower-cost organizations were not rewarded for their CQI efforts; they were penalized by lower reimbursement rates.

Many attempts to incorporate (integrate) this philosophy into these service industries continue today, often with good success. The lesson learned for innovation is one of both language and application. First, it requires the use of language that is innovation specific rather than industry specific; second, it requires reiteration that innovation is operationally independent, requiring a unique management strategy. Innovations are not processed; innovations are developed, evaluated, and validated.

For improving a process, use Six Sigma's DMAIC method (see Figure 2.1). The process works well with established operations, with specific defects associated with an identifiable problem. Six Sigma relies on systems theory as a backdrop.

The *process* requires inputs to operate (Figure 2.2). When the process completes a cycle, the process produces an output. Output is a tangible item or service evaluated for defects. Application of controls minimizes defects and improves output performance. Improvement occurs by minimizing defects, and the process operates at its expected level of performance. Typical projects include process re-engineering, ergonomics, customer (patient) satisfaction projects, and materials and purchasing management improvement. Six Sigma and Lean techniques are not in competition with innovation projects. The philosophy and resulting techniques provide a necessary strategy for most businesses and organizations. Assume that continuous improvement is an operational objective while innovation is a strategic objective.

Innovation operates with a different purpose—driven by meeting the needs, wants, and desires of individuals. After identifying the need, generating ideas, and selecting the best individuals for the innovation team, the team and management together create an objective. The objective is a time-bound goal that details the accomplishment. Innovations are next-generation products, services, or technology—not just

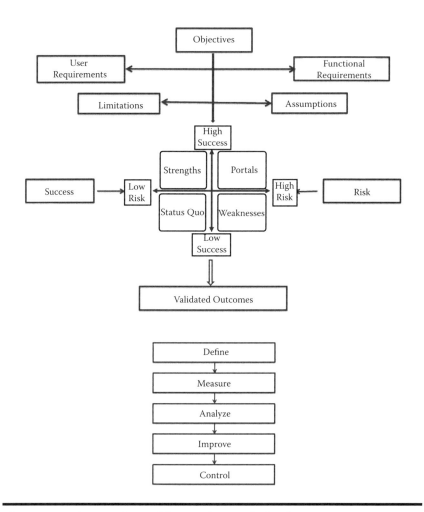

Figure 2.1 Comparison of innovation and Six Sigma processes. (Adapted from McLaughlin, G. and Caraballo, V., *Chance or Choice: Unlocking Innovation Success*, Taylor & Francis, Boca Raton, FL, 2013.)

Figure 2.2 Simple systems model.

improvements. Innovations transform a business or organization. Minimizing emergency room wait times may be an objective. For this minimization to become an innovation project, a specific and well-defined need must precede the formalization of the objective. The need may come from patients, regulatory bodies, or internal evidence collected over time. Whatever the need, this drives the objective. In addition, a time constraint must exist and an objective agreed upon by those in authority. This "buy-in" highlights its importance and level of support. A good example of creating a no-wait emergency department comes from the work of Jody Crane, MD, MBA and Chuck Noon, PhD (2011). Jody and his team used Lean tools as the basis for their process improvement project and included the use of basic and advanced flow techniques found in queuing theory combined with the theory of constraints. However, without administrative support and hard-wiring, the outcome of this project is not sustainable.

Figure 2.1 begins with the objective. An objective, combined with its functional and user requirements, constitutes an outcome. Outcomes are tangible descriptions (items) of what the innovation will accomplish. Assessment occurs combined with a statement of assumptions and limitations. The outcome becomes "innovative" after evaluating risk versus success. At this stage, the innovative outcome can begin the project implementation phase.

Obviously, innovation and continuous improvement operate at different levels and with a different purpose. Innovation operates outside normal daily routines. Effectively managing innovation requires a different strategy than that applied to daily operations. Use of a strategy applicable for other project implementations will certainly fail, given innovation's specific requirements, objectives, and assessments. Innovation requires a unique strategy for successful implementation. Piecing together a strategy that worked in the past is a risky alternative. This alternative exposes the outcome to chance, and this method proved successful only 10% of the time (deWaal, Martz, and Shieh, 2010). The cost of failure, false starts, and unrealized gains requires a more disciplined approach. To minimize risk, Global Targeting, Inc. developed, through testing and frequent assessment, a seven-step process to manage innovation prior to project implementation. An acronym, referred to as ENOVALE™ Solutions, identifies the seven-step process. Each letter represents a specific step in this process. Figure 2.3 identifies each key word in the process.

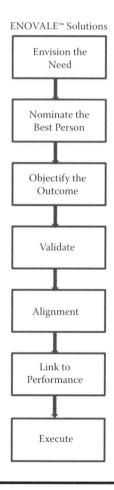

ENOVALE™ Solutions

Envision the Need

Nominate the Best Person

Objectify the Outcome

Validate

Alignment

Link to Performance

Execute

Figure 2.3   High-level innovation management: ENOVALE™ solutions. (Adapted from McLaughlin, G. and Caraballo, V., *Chance or Choice: Unlocking Innovation Success,* Taylor & Francis, Boca Raton, FL, 2013.)

Each stage or phase contains a detailed set of sub-steps. More information is available in *Chance or Choice: Unlocking Innovation Success* (McLaughlin and Caraballo, 2013a).

Innovation is more management strategy than operational process. In fact, *ENOVALE: How to Unlock Sustained Innovation Project Success* (McLaughlin and Caraballo, 2013b) explains the operational side of innovation.

Both methods involve a process with a distinctive purpose (innovation involves multiple processes). Both aid and facilitate the organization. Continuous improvement has an operations orientation, and innovation focuses on a growth orientation (sustained competitive advantage). Certainly, both methods share some tools and philosophy. Both strive for an improvement in recognizing the customer (patient) or user. Both benefit the organization. Innovation, however, understands what the customer (patient) needs and then delivers this need to satisfy long-term desires. Without innovation, everything maintains a status-quo state. With innovation, ideas enter the environment matching existing or unfulfilled needs, thus providing a mechanism for sustaining performance. Individuals evaluate this performance, recognize it as innovation (exceeds their expectations), and change purchase behaviors.

For innovation to function well within any organization, a supportive infrastructure must be present. Figure 2.4 details the innovation ecosystem. The infrastructure must support the People, Process, Customer, Technology, and the Extended Enterprise. ENOVALE is the framework used to accomplish innovation management.

To better understand ENOVALE, we developed a proven strategic process that works well within all sectors (including service businesses) and all functions. Figure 2.5 details the strategic components of innovation. Information (analytics) identifies and tracks needs, wants, or desires, thus permitting the creation of an innovative outcome. Balancing this information with the requirements that the business must meet creates the specific need and initial viability. The process of

Figure 2.4   Innovation ecosystem.

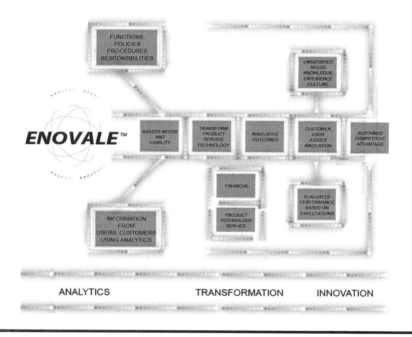

Figure 2.5   Global Targeting innovation model. (Adapted from McLaughlin and Caraballo, *ENOVALE: How to Unlock Sustained Innovation Project Success,* Taylor & Francis, Boca Raton, FL, 2013.)

transforming the product, service, or technology requires a blueprint for success—and that is ENOVALE!

ENOVALE is the method of institutionalizing innovation management. Once validated, the outcome transforms the organization to move from concept to reality. The transformation differs from process improvement, in that the patient (customer or end user) perceives and experiences the innovation. Experience and judgment enable the patient or customer to judge whether or not the item is innovative. Customers (patients) perceive the transformation as innovative if their needs are satisfied and if performance exceeds expectations. Ultimately, if innovation generates changes in consumer purchasing patterns, there is an opportunity for a sustained competitive advantage. That information flows back to the producer, who can further benefit from the change in consumer purchasing. This process links performance with innovation, creating a blueprint for success. This blueprint is what many have searched for, and the most significant contribution to date was made by Global Targeting, Inc.

An innovative item must satisfy needs and deliver superior performance. Improvements generated from continuous improvement efforts are occasionally innovative, using the definition described previously. The intent is not innovation, but rather improvement—a worthy goal. Innovations are generally rare, while improvements occur on a more frequent basis. Improvements are step-wise advances while innovations leap-frog the competition.

How Is Innovation Different?

Innovation is opportunity driven; continuous improvement is problem-driven. There will always be a need to identify, repair, or replace a defect. This need for continuous improvement is ongoing. Innovation does not replace this need but it does answer the need for continued growth through new opportunities. A healthy organization wants to grow, serve its patients well, and provide a reason for their loyalty and patronage. Innovation is not an "extension" of continuous improvement but rather an "expansion" of opportunities for the organization—which is particularly important during the implementation of the Patient Protection and Affordable Care Act (PPACA). The PPACA focuses on population health and payment reforms. Prior to 2014, physicians billed their office visits in levels 1 to 5, depending on the complexity of patient needs. These five levels were collapsed in 2014 to one level (CMS, 2013) for all types of visits, thus resulting in the need for innovation in care delivery.

In order for healthcare entities to survive, it requires more than just a philosophical shift; it requires a different management approach.

The natural next question is, how different? Briefly, management must do three things:

1. Release the innate talent within the organization.
2. Use the ethnic and cultural differences of the workforce as a springboard for innovative ideas.
3. Manage a process that converts ideas into opportunities that provide benefit to the organization.

Implementation of these requirements is difficult, taking up resources and time. Should management attempt to launch innovation without addressing these three requirements, failure is sure to come within 3 years or less. The reason for so bold a prediction is that research suggests (Dahl, Lawrence, and Pierce, 2011) that innovation programs generally last for 3 years or less in many organizations. A telltale sign that innovation efforts are not succeeding should signal problems ahead. Three indicators of potential failure are

1. A marked reduction in ongoing innovation projects (fewer employees involved)
2. Employees unaware of innovation successes or project status (internally, innovation is receiving less emphasis)
3. Reduced amounts of information (publicity) on innovation projects and successes released to the public (shareholders)

For simplicity, innovation is no longer the "flavor of the month." This scenario happened with CQI and Six Sigma. Truly, it is resistance to change. Innovation is inherently disruptive as it alters the status quo. Innovators do not "play it safe" but constantly "push the envelope." Organizations that recognize and reward this behavior easily accept innovation and create an environment that is open to new ideas. If innovation is present, it is recognizable through the workforce and products, services, or technology offered. You can feel the creative energy in the employees, management, and leadership. Creative organizations found that innovation focuses energy and individual efforts. The opposite is just as true. Those organizations that minimally innovate lack spontaneity, excitement is rare, and energy is controlled and subdued. Visionaries who see the potential of the workforce and find the resources to continue to challenge the competition by meeting the needs of the customer (patient) lead innovative organizations.

A definition of the end users and capturing their specific needs, wants, and desires is paramount (Figure 3.4). For the healthcare sector, this capture can be customer, user, patient, and professional. Resources that gather, filter, and interpret needs through data provide the building blocks for meeting needs, wants, and desires. Never assume that you have the knowledge to know what the end user wants, which is exactly why the CMS and The Joint Commission both require patient satisfaction data collection. Once collected, analytics is the field that captures this information and provides usable information. For much of the business-related healthcare sector, responsibility lies with the marketing department in conjunction with the quality department.

Global targeting recommends a repository for this information, using healthcare informaticists, and sharing this information with front-line managers. Every healthcare organization keeps patient and customer data on file and must make it ready for easy access by all managers. The mission of the organization must include the need for innovative products and services.

Summarizing the major differences that innovation generates:

Difference 1: The organization collects/catalogs needs, wants, and desires:
Identifying needs includes consumer, industry, and specialized information.

Difference 2: Transformation through ENOVALE:
Applying an innovation management process differently from daily operations.

Difference 3: Innovative outcomes:
Evaluating an idea/need for its risk-to-success ratio.

Difference 4: Validation:
Validating innovative outcomes before embarking on a project implementation.

Difference 5: Links to competitive or financial goals:
Establishing financial and performance success criteria prior to implementation.

These major differences demonstrate both the intensity and distinctiveness of innovation. Embarking on an innovation effort requires management, leadership, and support, as well as a mind-set change that recognizes that innovation requires a unique strategy. Management accepts the strategy as a choice or innovation becomes a chance occurrence.

Although differences exist, continuous quality improvement is a mainstay of successful operations. As innovative products mature (losing their innovative appeal), CQI may be a strategy for lengthening the product life cycle. One such area is evidence-based initiatives (EBIs). Launched as a disruptive innovation, improvement in both the products and science can continue with a CQI research paradigm (Rotheram-Borus, Swendeman, and Chorpita, 2012, p. 463). These EBIs are standard fare under the PPACA as value-based purchasing focuses on the implementation of evidence-based medicine. EBI is one example where innovation and continuous quality improvement overlap. There is a natural synergy between these two concepts. Again, continuous improvement is a necessity for success. However, innovation is a process used to leap-frog the competition. Achievement of this success requires a unique strategy for innovation.

Strategic Implications

Innovation will require a unique strategy, similar in many ways to a traditional operational strategy. A decision to innovate without first evaluating requirements, limitations, assumptions, and risk causes success to become a "crap shoot," leaving far too much to chance. Of course, there will be winners even with chance. Consider the marketing of state lotteries—someone has to win! Yet, a win every one in ten times is an expensive proposition. Improvement in those odds greatly benefits the organization. The best strategy is one that converts needs, wants, or desires into innovative outcomes.

The experiences of the authors over the past few years reveal a truth regarding innovation strategies in healthcare sector organizations. The truth is that innovation is more a goal than a strategy. In fact, leaders and managers are frequently unclear as to which direction to take. They know the need for innovation, but a clear implementation strategy eludes them. Many choose a particular technique such as "Blue Ocean" or "disruptive innovation" rather than creating a corporate strategy. When a corporate strategy does exist, it tends to cluster into one of two distinctive groups. These two groups behave more like tiers, one simple, one complex.

At present, an innovation strategy exists within an organization in two tiers (McLaughlin, 2012):

Tier 1

Loosely defined (innovation that is loosely tagged or nonexistent)

Special event (innovation due to a specific need or by random occurrence)

Departmentalized (i.e., R&D, assigned to a particular department)

Characteristics of Tier 1:

1. Innovation viewed as an event
2. Discussed and promoted with no strategic role
3. Inconsistent understanding of innovation
4. Responsibility at department level
5. Confused with design and development issues
6. Associated only with products or technology

Tier 2

Functional (functions like accounting, finance, and marketing)

Strategic (Chief Innovation Officer—plans and projects)

Integrated (full integration into the organizational culture and value system)

Characteristics of Tier 2:

1. Is strategic, that is, it is planned and funded
2. Operates throughout the organization, beginning at the individual level
3. Is fully integrated with functions similar to HR, finance, etc. (corporate-wide responsibility)
4. Is real-time with measured and managed metrics

Those organizations in Tier 2 understand the importance of innovation by integrating it into their organization. Tier 1 organizations (which tend to be the majority) still celebrate innovation as a special event and compartmentalize it to a department or group such as Research & Development. In a world where innovation is a key for success, Tier 1 organizations risk much.

Innovation at the strategic level must contain the following elements:

1. Corporate-wide effort to enable the presence of innovation in every department
2. Must be leader driven at the "C" level
3. Must be communicated to individuals and be receptive to feedback (customer, stakeholder)
4. Incorporate into company core values
5. Must be supported financially
6. Must be empirically based and objective driven

It is not enough to say that leadership supports innovation; leadership must be fully committed! Otherwise, efforts are sure to decline as interest declines.

There are a great many innovative activities in the health-care sector. Upon closer examination, most organizations would receive a Tier 1 classification, as expectations do not include innovative activities in all departments, only in those designated to create new products, technologies, and services.

Innovation occurs by chance and is often associated with a particular department or industry.

Leadership and management should be proactive toward innovation, moving from Tier 1 to Tier 2. Consider the following questions regarding the organization's present innovation strategy assessment:

1. Are innovation activities and projects evident in over 50% of departments?
2. How often does the topic of innovation come up in conversations?
3. Are directors, managers, and supervisors part of the corporate innovation strategy?
4. Is there a specific corporate strategy for innovation, or is it at the project level?
5. Do customers (patients) rate experience levels of performance that exceed their expectations?

Answering "No" to these questions places the organization in Tier 1 and at some risk. Obviously, environments that are more competitive must migrate from Tier 1 immediately. Less competitive (as much of the healthcare sector would be) environments should be migrating from Tier 1 to Tier 2.

Summary

The purpose of Chapter 2 was to explain the difference between innovation and other similar improvement projects/efforts. Innovation was examined in terms of philosophical approaches such as Total Quality, Continuous Improvement, and Six Sigma/Lean. Traditional improvement projects continue being worthwhile to the organization, providing recognizable improvements that affect bottom-line performance. Whereas these traditional programs reduce defects and inefficiencies, innovation directly affects customers (patients) by meeting an unrealized (unfulfilled) need while exceeding their expectations built over a period of years.

This chapter also examined the strategic elements of innovation, suggesting that a two-tier system exists. Tier 1 innovation is spontaneous, and is not a planned event; Tier 2 is planned as a strategic element with corporate support and resources. Organizations that incorporate innovation as a key strategic element will benefit greatly from this endeavor. If the organization combines both Tier 1 and Tier 2 elements, then the efforts focus on migrating to Tier 2 as quickly as possible.

This chapter provided an introduction to the ENOVALE methodology and to Global Targeting, Inc.'s innovation process management.

The enactment of the Patient Protection and Affordable Care Act (in 2010) provides a rare opportunity to use the ENOVALE innovation technique to meet the new payment demands for population health. The Act includes monies for setting up "medical homes" designed to coordinate the care of individuals with an outcome of improving the overall health of the population. Successful organizations will use this technique to access monies for innovation and will succeed using these proven techniques.

Discussion Questions

1. In an effort to improve the patient experience, improve outcomes, and decrease costs for care, healthcare leaders used several techniques including total quality management, continuous improvement, and Six Sigma/Lean. These techniques provided varying results. Support the need to use innovation techniques today.

2. Several organizations incorporated innovation centers into their offerings: The Centers for Medicare & Medicaid Services, the American Medical Association, the American Hospital Association, and the American Organization of Nurse Executives. Review one of their innovation websites

and discuss how they fit with the current need for innovation.

Assignments

Identify a healthcare product, process, service, or technology that satisfies an unfulfilled need. If you were managing the project, develop an objective based on the need identified. Establish five to eight minimum requirements (both user and functional), and all necessary assumptions and limitations. From this, create an innovative outcome. Once complete, answer the following questions:

1. How would you minimize risk to the receiver, such as a patient?
2. How would you validate such an innovative outcome?
3. How would you align stakeholders (employees, suppliers, customers) to accepting and purchasing (using) the innovation?
4. What type of performance would indicate that this item is superior to that of competitors?
5. Would you vote to move this project forward?

Chapter 3

Healthcare Professionals Survey Results

Introduction

Since Florence Nightingale's initial studies on sanitation and patient practices, nurse executives have followed in her footsteps to create policies and procedures, and conducted evidence-based research for the basis of nursing protocols. Following the esteemed research of Nightingale, the American Nurses Association (ANA) conducted research and identified nursing-sensitive indicators, which demonstrate the effect of nursing care on patient outcomes (American Nurses Association, n.d.). Further, the ANA outlines standards for this future research, which ultimately represents nursing's commitment to research and innovation. Based on this historical commitment from nursing, a representative sample of nurse executives from the American Organization of Nurse Executives (AONE) was surveyed to determine their readiness and ability to innovate.

The survey was designed by Global Targeting, Inc. to assess how organizational leadership understands and recognizes innovation. The authors wanted to select a typical health-care sector organization that would provide an in-depth understanding of how members perceive innovation. Realizing the immensity of this sector, this survey provides a "snapshot" of perceptions involving innovation. The authors selected the AONE (American Organization of Nursing Executives) as that representative organization.

The AONE (www.aone.org) agreed to participate in the survey with 163 members completing the survey. The purpose of this survey was to understand how AONE members perceived innovation and its practical application and implications for the healthcare sector. The survey measured perceptions of innovation, the respondent's work environment, and values normally associated with innovation. In addition, respondents provided demographic information and information on what elements they deemed necessary for a successful and sustained innovation effort.

Prior to its availability, the AONE broadcast its intention to sponsor the conduction of the survey through its Research Committee. The survey was made available to AONE members during the fall of 2013. Analysis consisted of 195 survey responses.

The innovation survey was an adaptation of a survey constructed and validated in 1999 (Zhuang, 1995; Zhuang, Williamson, and Carter, 1999) and then again modified by Caraballo and McLaughlin in 2012. The work environment and innovation values surveys are the work of McLaughlin and Caraballo (2013a) and are both validated and reliable. This particular innovation survey determines how an individual understands and identifies innovation. Three distinctive characteristics (constructs) emerge from the survey: identification of new, improved, and changed (different from the original) innovation. Individuals identify innovation as either something that is unique (new), improved, or changed significantly. Individuals recognize innovation in three unique applications, only one of which is an "invention - new."

For AONE members, this outcome is a significant finding. Innovation exists beyond new technologies providing a service

that is much improved, a product with accelerated performance, or a change of personnel that encourages positive
outcomes. Given the very nature of healthcare, from design to
process to outcome, customers (patients) and users can easily
recognize innovation. In addition, the survey measured attitudes regarding the work environment best suited for innovative outcomes and sustained innovation success.

Finally, comparing different demographic groups (gender,
function, age, and experience) provided an interesting cultural
contrast. Although agreement is widespread, there was enough
of a discrepancy that the AONE can provide a leadership role
in recognizing and encouraging innovation within the healthcare industry.

Methodology and Demographic Analysis

Methodology

The AONE Member Innovation survey contained both perceptual and factual questions. Analysis of perceptual statements included descriptive statistics and factor analysis (SPSS
Version 19) with varimax rotation. The purpose was to determine if the three hypothesized components of innovation were
present. In addition, details of the components of the work
environment and value assignment scores were completed by
respondents. Demographic group analysis helped explain some
of the differences identified. Factor analysis provided ongoing
information on content, face, and predictive validity for survey
analysis. In addition, a Chrobach alpha (reliability analysis)
yielded scores that all far exceeded the minimum requirements
of 0.70. An ANOVA (analysis of variance), on the ten innovation
statement scores, confirmed a statistical difference between
question responses at the .05 level of significance. For non-
survey questions (statements), descriptive charts and graphs
provided information on respondent choices.

Demographic Analysis

Exactly 195 AONE members participated in the innovation survey. Females greatly outnumbered males in this sample. A comparison between genders is not possible, given the small sample size for males (Figure 3.1). This result is predictable, given the historical dominance of women in the nursing profession.

Next, age differences were examined (Figure 3.2). The majority of respondents who participated were either "Baby Boomers" or those in "Generation X." Few older individuals or younger nursing professionals participated in the survey.

Occupation or job description is also of value (Figure 3.3). The data indicates a diversity of positions and responsibilities

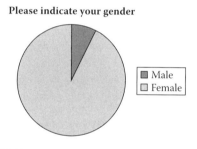

Figure 3.1   Gender differences: AONE survey. (From Global Targeting, Inc., Chicago, IL. With permission.)

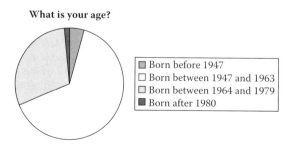

Figure 3.2   Age categorizations. (From Global Targeting, Inc., Chicago, IL. With permission.)

Which category best describes your position?

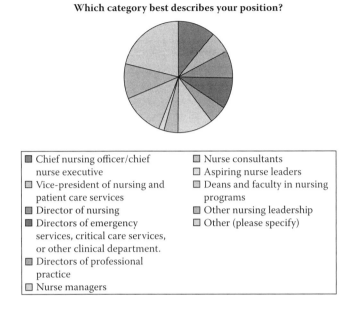

■ Chief nursing officer/chief nurse executive	□ Nurse consultants
□ Vice-president of nursing and patient care services	□ Aspiring nurse leaders
■ Director of nursing	□ Deans and faculty in nursing programs
■ Directors of emergency services, critical care services, or other clinical department.	■ Other nursing leadership
■ Directors of professional practice	□ Other (please specify)
□ Nurse managers	

Figure 3.3   Industry occupation AONE members (From Global Targeting, Inc. Chicago, IL. With permission.)

within the organization. Director and above levels tend to be more prevalent than manager roles. This differentiation provided an excellent evaluation, as leaders tended to dominate the sample size collected. Leadership is critical for sustained innovation success. Their perceptions will help lead the effort and also set the tone and emphasis of innovation activities throughout the organization. Research (Caraballo and McLaughlin, 2012) showed that age and position (job function) affect how innovation is perceived and rated in importance. Each age group uses a different "lens" to examine, identify, and categorize innovation.

An additional demographic variable, highest degree earned (Figure 3.4), also presented a diverse background for respondents. There is almost an even split between those with an MSN (Master of Science in Nursing) degree and those without this degree. These respondents well represent both leadership and a well-educated professional.

What is your highest level of education?

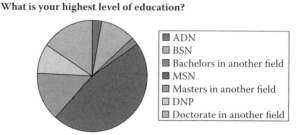

Figure 3.4   Respondents' educational achievements. (From Global Targeting, Inc., Chicago, IL. With permission.)

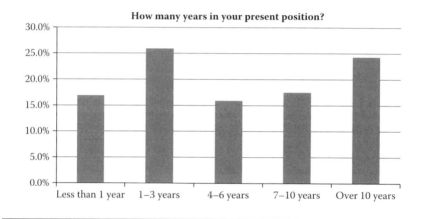

Figure 3.5   Years within their present position. (From Global Targeting, Inc., Chicago, IL. With permission.)

There is a variety of experience within this group. Figure 3.5 shows that there is a relatively equal number of respondents in both short-term and long-term commitments. Again, the representation to the overall healthcare sector is reassuring. Therefore, respondents are generally from the United States, have earned a high level of education, and are presently in a leadership or managerial role. Given this general demographic, individuals experienced exposure to innovation, and for those in healthcare, included experience with both long- and short-term life-cycle innovations. Experience, application, and industry involvement affect overall innovation perceptions.

For the healthcare sector, which is industrial based, short t innovations are the lifeblood of the organization. The question remains as to whether the organizational infrastructure is accommodating or resisting these short life cycles. Unless the organization implements a specific strategy that promotes innovation, numerous attempts to innovate will fail.

While most respondents reside in the United States, there is a possibility that cultural influences may also affect the perceptions of innovation. This influence is considered small, given the association's general purpose.

Perceptions of Innovation

Individuals perceive innovation based on their experiences and knowledge of past performances. Innovation is present when perceptions greatly exceed expectations. Since perceptions will vary, so does the number of definitions of innovation. Therefore, rather than defining innovation specifically, the authors use the "means of innovation." The "means of innovation" are the transformations made to product, service, or technology that individuals identify as innovative (Baregheh et al., 2009). Researchers identified these "means of innovation" as three distinct themes or concepts of innovation. Each concept or theme describes the way or "means" of identifying an innovative product, service, or technology. Respondents can then classify whether the innovation meets or improves their existing needs. For example, stocks, bonds, or commodities comprise methods or ways to invest money. All accomplish the same goal (hopefully). Each investment type requires a unique (and often related) strategy. Innovation follows the same pattern; it begins and ends with the individual. If we experience something better than what we expect and it satisfies more of our needs, then we say it is innovative. The perception of innovativeness increases as more needs are satisfied. These themes represent both the tangible and intangible assessment of innovation. The three themes of innovation become

Theme 1: **New** (something new or a novel [unique] idea): Normally we think of new technology.

Theme 2: **Improvement** (making a product, service, or technology better): This relates to products, processes, or services. Improvement in performance is for outsourcing products, processes, or services. This is the most common outcome of innovation in the healthcare sector.

Theme 3: **Change** (replacing what presently exists with something better): This affects people both physically and emotionally. Innovative change is positive change benefiting the organization.

Table 3.1 lists the means and standard devistions for this AONE data. Respondents rate each question on an agreement scale from 1 (Strongly Disagree) to 5 (Strongly Agree). Any average over 4.0 is a positive assessment of the innovation component. Variation is relatively stable, except for Question "g."

Using confirmatory factor analysis, these three themes of innovation were validated for all cultural groups studied to date (Project Impact Institute). This research confirms the findings that the three themes (means of innoavtion) best describe innovation.

For the AONE respondents, the perceptions of innovation were factored by gender, age, and position (Table 3.1). Because the sample size for men is small (only 16 replied), the analysis is somewhat indefinite for such a small sample size. All other demographics were combined (female and male data).

The strength factor measures (Figure 3.6) the degree of agreement with a particular theme. Overall, the most common identifier is improvement, followed by change and new. Upon review, there were a number of interesting results.Only two age cohorts (Baby Boomers, born from 1946 to 1963) and

Table 3.1   Descriptive Statistics: Innovation

	Mean	Std. Deviation	Analysis N
a. Inventing something entirely new	4.0368	0.91550	163
b. Generating new ideas	4.4969	0.60220	163
c. Improving something that already exists	4.3436	0.67018	163
d. Enhancing the desirability of something	4.0429	0.84144	163
e. "Thinking out of the box"	4.5460	0.56876	163
f. Taking something that already exists and making it better	4.3374	0.67788	163
g. Changing the technology by making the previous version obsolete	3.4417	1.05467	163
h. Adopting something that has been tried elsewhere	3.5337	0.94465	163
i. Using a different perspective	4.2025	0.68637	163
j. Introducing changes to make something better	4.2883	0.70030	163

Source: Global Targeting, Inc., Chicago, IL. With permission.

Demographics			Strength Factor		
Position	Generation	Gender	1	2	3
		M	New/Improve	Change/New	
		F	Improve	New	Change
	Gen X		Improve	New	Change
	Baby Boomers		Improve	Change	New
Nurse Leadership			Change	Improve	New
Nurse Managers			Improve	New	Change

Figure 3.6   Innovation alignment matrix: AONE innovation survey.

(Generation X, born from 1964 to 1980) contained enough of a sample to do a statistical comparison. The results provided a great deal of agreement bewteen the age groups except for the emphasis on "new" for the younger AONE members. Research (Caraballo and McLaughlin, 2012) determined that younger respondents tend to place "new" as their first choice.

The most interesting dichtomy is the difference between Nurse Leaders and Nurse Managers, suggesting a very different approach to innovation. This difference could cause friction or misunderstandings if the type of innovation desired is not clearly identified. When combined with differences in age, the result suggests that innovation could be misunderstood.

Statement numbers in bold (Table 3.2) constitute when Nurse Leaders and Managers held a different perception of innovation. Statements 3 and 4 describe elements of "Improve" rated significantly different, confirming the dichotomy that

Table 3.2   ANOVA Analysis of Survey Statements when Differentiating for Job Position

Tests of Between-Subjects Effects						
Source	*Dependent Variable*	*Type III Sum of Squares*	*df*	*Mean Square*	*F*	*Sig.*
	Statement 1	.638	1	.638	.756	.386
	Statement 2	.008	1	.008	.028	.868
	Statement 3	**3.021**	**1**	**3.021**	**7.112**	**.009**
	Statement 4	**4.827**	**1**	**4.827**	**7.799**	**.006**
	Statement 5	1.103	1	1.103	3.408	.067
	Statement 6	1.051	1	1.051	2.541	.113
	Statement 7	1.379	1	1.379	1.207	.274
	Statement 8	.006	1	.006	.006	.938
	Statement 9	.038	1	.038	.078	.780
	Statement 10	**3.118**	**1**	**3.118**	**6.402**	**.013**

exists. Leadership perceives "Change" as being the more dynamic means of innovation, while managers understand that "Improvement" is most evident. When comparing averages, it is critical to understand that these statistics are measures of central tendency only and do not represent the spread of responses across the AONE member responses. These differences, however, confirm that varying perceptions exist for innovation, and that innovation is best determined at the individual level. That is, individuals use their experience with the performance of a product, service, or technology to judge innovation.

Given the diversity of perceptions, one obvious outcome is the importance of the message to patients (customers) and users, as well as its presentation and comprehension. Clarity, cohesiveness, and directed information (based on expected knowledge and experience) are all critical elements. Processing and understanding the message is critical for providers, including the meeting of needs and the "transformation" of the product, service, or technology to fit the message. Communications, marketing, and advertising are effective "transformations," assuming the innovation outperforms its predecessor. Innovation is not easy but it is now achievable because the provider's knowledge now exceeds that of its direct competitors.

Other Factors Affecting Innovation

No examination of how individuals understand innovation was conducted; however, respondents were requested to describe their work environment, values, benefits of innovation, organizational factors needed to initiate innovation, etc. A positive work environment encourages innovation. However, innovation's individual emphasis also depends on the attitude and demeanor of the respondent. A positive outlook certainly enables the individual to be open to the innovation process.

Work Environment

The survey asked respondents to characterize their work environment. A confirmatory factor analysis identified up to three distinctive factors or concepts (Figure 3.7). Males and female Nurse Executives and Managers viewed the environment differently, especially in assessing their own ability and confidence. What is most interesting lies in the different perceptions of the word "demand": men see it favorably (+ word demand) and women unfavorably (− work demand). Both are competent workers; it is in their perceptions of its effect on the work environment that are different.

Generational cohort also exhibited a difference (male and female respondents combined) as Generation X respondents perceived work demands and challenges as separate (independent) contributors to an evaluation of the work environment. The Baby Boomers tended to combine these and perceive it as contributing as a collective to the overall work

Demographics			Strength Factor		
Position	Generation	Gender	1	2	3
		M	Positive Workplace Attitude	Challenges, Confidence, New Ideas	Cooperation and (+) Work Demands
		F	Positive Workplace Attitude	Challenges, Confidence, (−) Work Demands	
	Gen X		Positive Workplace Attitude	(+) Work Demands	Challenges
	Baby Boomers		Positive Workplace Attitude	Challenges, Confidence, (−) Work Demands	
Nurse Leadership			Positive Workplace Attitude	Challenges, Confidence, (−) Work Demands	
Nurse Managers			Positive Workplace Attitude	Confidence	Challenges and (−) Work Demands

Figure 3.7   Factor analysis: Work environment patterns. (From Global Targeting, Inc. Chicago, IL. With permission.)

environment. Because perceptions relate to beliefs, a different perspective of one group to another could be determined as potential nonalignment.

Finally, Nurse Leadership collectively sees issues of work demand and confidence in one's ability to solve problems as a more personal trait. Nurse Managers perceive the unique characteristic of confidence in one's ability to solve problems as separate from work demand issues. Although these groups seem similar, the subtle differences underlie an evaluation of the work environment as one that is separable by personal issues. Leaders could judge managers as weaker or less effective due to the issue of confidence.

Values Assessment of Innovation

Much like the assessment of the work environment, identification about what AONE members value concerning innovation is important. A ten-item set of survey statements measured the perceptions of what is valued during an innovation effort.

The two main components are project concerns (time, cost, number of people involved) and the innovation potential (new, improvement, and change). Depending on how one judges the value of innovation, a different perspective can arise. Some value the project essentials (time, cost, and personnel), while others value the actual innovation benefit itself. It is obvious to see that if one values the innovation and another the value of resources applied to the innovation, then a difference in understanding could occur. Given that AONE members share differing views, this dichotomy suggests that innovation within organizations is valued quite differently.

Figure 3.8 shows that cost, time, and participant resources are first, with innovation potential as secondary. The complexity in understanding what one values directly relates to one's preferences and choices. For AONE, there is agreement

Demographics			Strength Factor		
Position	Generation	Gender	1	2	3
		M	Costs, Time, and People	Innovation Potential	
		F	Costs, Time, and Change/Improvement	People, Novelty	
	Gen X		Costs, Time, and People	Innovation Potential	
	Baby Boomers		Costs, Time, Improvement Potential	People, Novelty Change	
Nurse Leadership			Costs, Time, and People	Innovation Potential	
Nurse Managers			Costs, Time, and People	Change and Technology	Improvement and Novelty

Figure 3.8 Innovation values assessment. (From Global Targeting, Inc., Chicago, IL. With permission.)

that innovations must produce value (whether in cost savings, efficiencies, or improvements), and that concerns of time and personnel affect any decision. The agreement as to what is valued by the respondents to this survey indicates that these professionals can easily see the potential of innovation and come to a quick and decisive decision.

Who benefits most from innovation?

Although the individual receives less positive scores, it is positive (Figure 3.9). Innovation benefits everyone in the organization, especially the patients. Figure 3.10 details which group or function is best suited for initiating innovation. Leadership is given the most credibility, while those "front line" positions seem to be the least likely. What is interesting is that those individuals in direct contact with patients (customers) seem least likely to initiate innovation. This fact may be one of many reasons that patients (customers) seem to be the last to experience innovative products, services, or technology. This outcome could be one element of improvement of interest in the future.

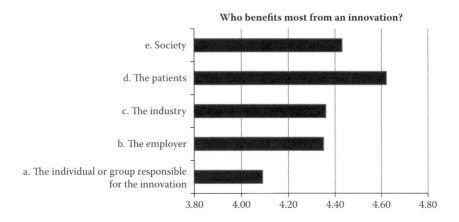

Figure 3.9   Who benefits most from innovation?

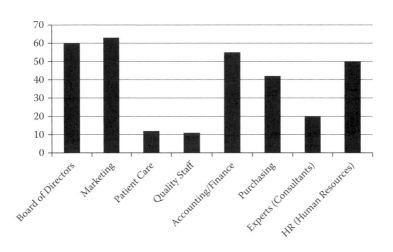

Figure 3.10   Best position to initiate innovation.

Critical Reasons for Innovation

Individuals identify possible innovation outcomes in their organizations: that is, the critical reasons for embarking into innovation. Figure 3.11 shows that challenging competitors is the primary reason for initiating innovation projects. Second, it is to reduce the effect of decreased reimbursements. Third, cost containment and regulatory pressures affect when

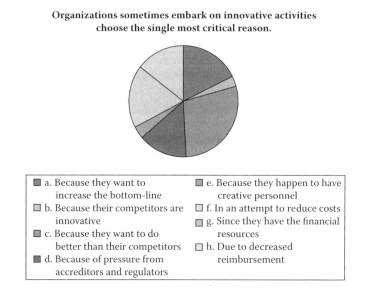

Organizations sometimes embark on innovative activities
choose the single most critical reason.

□ a. Because they want to increase the bottom-line
□ b. Because their competitors are innovative
□ c. Because they want to do better than their competitors
□ d. Because of pressure from accreditors and regulators
□ e. Because they happen to have creative personnel
□ f. In an attempt to reduce costs
□ g. Since they have the financial resources
□ h. Due to decreased reimbursement

Figure 3.11 Critical reasons for innovation activities. (From Global Targeting, Inc., Chicago, IL. With permission.)

innovation projects are not taken. All other benefits are small in comparison. This outcome, then, solidifies the objective for innovations.

In a traditional setting, innovation, as a competitive tool, is its prime purpose. In the healthcare sector, there are numerous influences such as reducing disbursements and regulatory concerns. These will drive the innovation efforts. Yet, innovation comes from unrealized needs. Therefore, these needs may be the issues listed or other yet unknown issues. Recognition of the need is as critical as developing the innovative item.

From the business side of this sector, keeping ahead of competitors is critical in a business that changes rapidly. This paradigm requires not only a positive response to change, but also highlights the need for a proactive, positive work environment. Once the objective for innovation activities is clear, the organization can incorporate innovation as a viable strategy. This data analysis clearly states that this objective is the end goal for innovation. Of course, this view is from the perceptions of AONE members, not those who receive the project, service, or technology. Their view of innovation comes from experience with the item, deciding whether it meets an unrealized need, and how it performs—does it meet or exceed expectations (Figure 3.11).

Personal Abilities Needed for Innovation Success

Interestingly, AONE members think that creative thinking is the most important individual attribute for innovation. Figure 3.12 displays those skills needed to be innovative, as judged by the respondents. Creativity is a key for innovation when specific needs apply. Idea generation in itself is marginally effective. When combined with a needs analysis, the resulting outcome contains both perceived value and defined benefit. Creativity or ideation (idea generation) must come after the establishment of the need. There are many excellent texts and training programs for creating ideas. The critical element is to establish a need and then let the creative energies flow during the process of creating the innovative outcome. Even individuals who do not consider themselves creative will participate when the need is clearly established. Although the

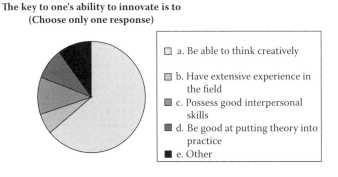

Figure 3.12 Personal abilities needed for innovation success. (From Global Targeting, Inc., Chicago, IL. With permission.)

respondents choose creativity, anyone can innovate when the need is immediate.

The creativity process is always a critical tool throughout the innovation process, but especially when producing a new or novel innovation (ones never tried before). Responses from AONE members agree well with previous research data.

Organizational Activities Needed to Realize One's Innovation Potential

To realize an individual's potential, certain organizational factors must be present. The AONE members evaluated a number of organizational factors that must be present to realize one's innovation potential. By examining Figure 3.13, AONE members identified two critical factors: (1) encouragement to take risks and (2) freedom to work in areas of greatest interest. These choices are consistent with previous research involving highly technical groups. Leadership must ensure that risk

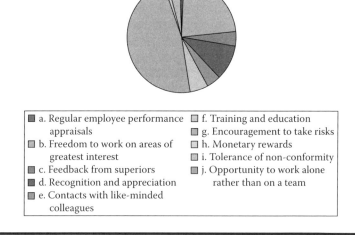

Organizational factors paramount to realizing one's innovation potential

- a. Regular employee performance appraisals
- b. Freedom to work on areas of greatest interest
- c. Feedback from superiors
- d. Recognition and appreciation
- e. Contacts with like-minded colleagues
- f. Training and education
- g. Encouragement to take risks
- h. Monetary rewards
- i. Tolerance of non-conformity
- j. Opportunity to work alone rather than on a team

Figure 3.13 Organizational factors in realizing one's innovation potential. (From Global Targeting, Inc., Chicago, IL. With permission.)

taking is rewarded and provide the time for employees to work on special projects.

Most of the factors listed in Figure 3.13 contribute to permitting individuals to dedicate time and effort to innovative activities. Interestingly, past studies, using employees, highlighted recognition, feedback, and training and education as highly rated. This discovery suggests that position and possibly industry may dictate how and why an individual chooses to participate in the innovation process. The divergence in perceptions does indicate a potential roadblock to achieving innovation excellence.

Organizational Factors Most Emphasized

Complementing the previous analysis, organizational factors from the business view can easily initiate innovation. From the organizational perspective, businesses use many factors (see Figure 3.14) to initiate innovation. When businesses

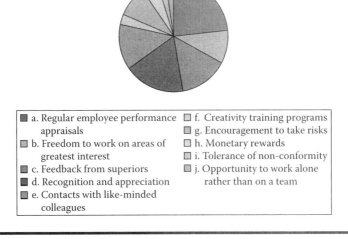

Which organizational factor do you think is most emphasized in the organization where you work? (choose only one response)

■ a. Regular employee performance appraisals
■ b. Freedom to work on areas of greatest interest
■ c. Feedback from superiors
■ d. Recognition and appreciation
■ e. Contacts with like-minded colleagues
☐ f. Creativity training programs
☐ g. Encouragement to take risks
☐ h. Monetary rewards
☐ i. Tolerance of non-conformity
■ j. Opportunity to work alone rather than on a team

Figure 3.14 Organizational factors emphasized in business. (From Global Targeting, Inc., Chicago, IL. With permission.)

emphasize factors that can clash with the individual's per-spective, innovation can greatly suffer. A disconnect occurs if individuals desire the freedom to work on projects that inter-est them but the organization offers only recognition or some minor reward.

Complementary factors will provide the most beneficial impetus to innovation. In both cases, the freedom to work on areas of greatest interest and risk-taking are key factors that individuals use to be innovative.

Summary

The AONE innovation survey provides a unique perspective on how members perceive innovation. Individual perceptions of innovation may vary, depending on a respondent's health-care sector perspective. These differences may provide a unique opportunity to "close the gap" between individuals and management. Rewarding what benefits the individual and the business is a definite "win-win" situation! Organizations that can tailor their efforts to support the individual, while meet-ing company objectives, increase their chance of success. As Global Targeting, Inc. constantly states, "Innovation begins and ends with the individual." If AONE members take this to heart and devise strategies that support the individual and the sec-tor, then innovation will become a sustained reality.

There is a tremendous amount of agreement that financial aspects regarding an innovation project are as critical as its overall potential. However, emphasizing one of the aspects (values on time, costs, and human resources) without acknowl-edging or rewarding the other (the innovation potential) would spell disaster. By ignoring a value, an individual's attitude and productivity decrease. If businesses and organizations' leaders begin placing value on both concerns (financial and potential), individuals will align themselves to shared values. Alignment of individuals is critical for innovation success.

The positive work environment that members of the AONE described is also critical for success. Again, agreement between upper management and employees on which aspects define a positive work environment is required before embarking on an innovation project. Do not assume that alignment already exists; evaluate it before you begin. Employees want cooperation, collaboration, and trust. These workplace attitudes become the work "environment" in which innovation can flourish.

What is most important to remember is that AONE members possess diversified perceptions of innovation, work environment, and values. The authors attempted to classify these for gender, age, and position. Even with these categories, the diversity in perceptions is noteworthy. As a professional organization, it may be helpful to define innovation (or the means of innovation as we do at Global Targeting, Inc.). Look for instances where shared values are accepted and a priority for all members. We encourage members to consider a more global perspective on innovation, one that provides benefit for the individual *and* the organization. Define innovation in terms of who and what receives a benefit. The diversity (variation) in response is an opportunity to solidify innovation and its requirements for a successful implementation.

Discussion Questions

1. What can you conclude by respondent participants if reward and benefits existed openly for those professional nursing employees?
2. Why do you believe that being given the time to be creative (innovative) (Figure 3.12) is critical for healthcare employees in their innovation efforts?
3. Would you conclude that all nursing professionals believe that innovation is doable as a strategy in the organization in which they are employed?

Assignments

1. After reading this chapter, summarize the results. Create a one-page Executive Summary detailing the results and any recommendations or suggestions you may have to offer.
2. Explain what it signifies if innovation is not easily subdivided into three unique components. Consider factors such as: age, function, and gender differences.
3. Explain what it means for the nursing profession when individuals recommend that "thinking creatively" is the most important characteristic needed for successful innovation.

Chapter 4

Understanding Sustained Innovation: The Concept of Originality

Introduction

Sustaining innovation throughout the organization in the healthcare sector requires a fundamental understanding of the needs of the customer or patient. Given the changing environment, will opportunities be medical breakthroughs, patient-focused approaches, or cost-focused efforts? With decreasing reimbursement, focus on population health and value-based purchasing, the efforts need to focus on changing how care occurs, including reducing waste in both human resources and materials, avoiding duplication and unnecessary tests, and early intervention. Innovation opportunities must flow from these needs. Chapter 2 described the research efforts of Global Targeting, Inc. and how individual perceptions of innovation fall into three categories: new, improved, and change. Chapter 3 relied on the innovation model to explain the transformation from need to outcome to innovation reality. Chapter 4 describes how originality affects the decision to proceed with innovation. The staggering cost of creating a breakthrough product or technology may limit its possibility. Therefore, those in the healthcare sector need to devise opportunities for innovation. Originality occupies three distinctive states for innovation: for new items, for new applications, and for new approaches. This chapter discusses these aspects of originality, within the healthcare sector as a guide.

Often, need requires new or unique opportunities (outcomes). These outcomes are original, new solutions never implemented, much like an invention or a new discovery. This type of innovation requires "out-of-the-box thinking" and creativity or ideation (idea generation) skills. There are few obstacles to creating new ideas (Anonymous, 2003), except for the number, disposition, and implementation of such ideas. For instance, cancer and infections spread through the lymph nodes and make it harder to eliminate. Recently, researchers found a way to deliver medication specifically to the lymph nodes (Liu et al., 2014). These kinds of breakthroughs improve intervention and decrease the amount of medication needed, which decreases suffering and the costs of care.

According to an article in *The Futurist*, most ideas that drive innovation come from outside the workplace (Anonymous, 2003). Removal of individuals from the work environment increases their creativity, especially at this stage where originality is critical. Ideation will generate ideas that are more useful once the need is established. For innovation ideas that never existed previously, the idea (or truly the inspiration) will often precede the need (think smartphone and iPad®)—these are special situations, not planned or organized. These events happen without a timetable or without a plan. The frequency and predictability of these events is unknown; therefore, planning is not an issue. As an organization, be open (like Apple) to these events but plan as if innovation is manageable.

Far too often, individuals understand innovation only as an invention, yet innovation can flourish when understood in a broader context. Innovation has the capacity to change the organization, reset the life cycle, and shift the existing paradigm. The key to capturing innovation in the organization derives from creating a culture where leadership supports innovation and recognizes the potential of individuals to innovate.

Originality as a Key Differentiator

The definition of originality refers to the amount of uniqueness present in a product, process, technology, or service. For the sake of simplicity, the product, process, service, or technology is referred to as an "item." The more original an item, the more distinctiveness, creativity, and newness it acquires. "New" items can come about because of the presence or availability of existing components, hardware, and technology. Understanding the concept or theme of "new" requires a better development of the word "originality." Therefore, there are four levels of originality:

Level 1: Originality: uses no existing resources or technology, is unique; a good example is the discovery of penicillin.

Level 2: Originality: an item uses existing resources and/or technology, has no predecessor; the pacemaker for the heart is an excellent example.

Level 3: Originality: an item is new by version or use (application); third- or fourth-generation CAT scan, for example.

Level 4: Originality: an item is new by approach (an existing item applied or marketed differently); an example would be using aspirin to help control aspects of heart disease.

The first level of originality includes items that have never existed. These could be items such as a new discovery or invention. A new vaccine is an example of a Level 1, since it has never existed in the past. A Level 2 innovation builds on existing knowledge and resources. A good example would be a re-engineered antibiotic that can fight infections more aggressively.

The iPad is a new version of the tablet computer (Level 3); most innovations are actually Level 3 originality items. An example of Level 3 innovation in healthcare involves the use of apps for the iPad. These apps allow providers to monitor a patient's health status by sending critical information from the app to a provider. It provides an opportunity to intervene early to keep the patient healthy. New opportunities for provider apps include adding to the "internet of things" (every-day objects connected to a network and work together—Oxford Dictionary) by creating programs that work synchronously with computer chips embedded into medical devices (Baum, 2014a).

Level 4 items include new uses of an existing item. For example, pre-operative risk assessment was done on paper using the SF-36® Health Survey to gather information about the patient. Now, the risk assessment is combined electronically with the patient's electronic history. The new outcome is a calculated level of risk connected to the procedure with a determination of the appropriateness of the procedure for the specific patient. In addition, it takes into consideration specialty guidelines. The final step is adding the risk calculation to the patient's informed consent form for discussion with the patient (Baum, 2014b).

Discoveries and unique inventions (Level 1) occur infrequently and thereby are more difficult to produce. Level 2 describes an item that is "new" to the user, using existing components, technology, or available resources (example: the sonogram). Level 3 focuses on a new application using an item for a different purpose (example: cell phones with built-in camera). Finally, Level 4, the easiest to replicate, is a new approach using resources in a different combination (example: adding an anti-bacterial agent into a hand washing solution). Levels 2-4 are simpler and occur more frequently since the resources and technology exist (see Figure 4.1). Yet, all levels of originality are "new" to the user who experiences an item. The key to longevity is Levels 1 and 2.

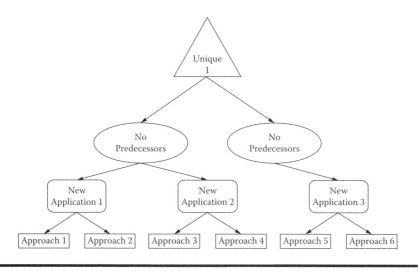

Figure 4.1 Levels of originality. (From Global Targeting, Inc., Chicago, IL. With permission.)

Using the descriptor "new" implies a sense of freshness, distinctiveness, and "cutting-edge." The announcement of new pharmaceutical products, new medical technologies, and new breakthroughs meets Level 2 criteria. It not only provides financial rewards, but also brings prestige and a distinct competitive advantage. Research and Development organizations develop processes to move Level 1 and 2 ideas (and needs) to implementation. This process applies to new products and new technology. However, a process to implement a Level 1 or 2 idea/need for a service-oriented organization is nonexistent. An ENOVALE™ process exists to manage the creation and validation of innovative services. More detail is available in *ENOVALE: How to Unlock a Sustained Innovation Project Success* (McLaughlin and Caraballo, 2013b). Service businesses can easily operate on all levels of originality. To accomplish this effectively, service- and patient-oriented organizations must undergo a paradigm shift. That is, they must develop an innovation management strategy using ENOVALE as a backdrop for success.

Can Originality Benefit the Healthcare Organization and Professional Outside of R&D?

The most overlooked include Levels 3 and 4, which can pro-vide tremendous opportunity. For example, over 10 years ago, GE Medical was looking for an opportunity to sell imaging devices in South America. Unfortunately, the price was beyond the means of most purchasers. GE Medical made a practice of not selling used (older model) devices. During a series of negotiations, the South American reseller asked if the company could sell recent, refurbished machines. GE Medical agreed, as this resell market would not violate their long-standing rule. South Americans received a refurbished machine at a discount price, thus permitting more patients to make use of this innovative device. A new use (application) for these machines enabled both parties to achieve a successful outcome (personal experience).

The third type of "new" identifies a new approach. Much of the healthcare community uses a new approach on a frequent basis. Take a simple example: supplying prescriptions to patients with a 90-day versus a 30-day supply. At first, this is a very innovative approach, and pleasing to the patient. Innovation exceeds the customer's (patient's) expectations. Patient satisfaction increases, resulting in a change in purchasing behaviors. However, the competition easily copied the approach, leaving the net benefits short-lived. New approaches often have a limited "shelf life"; implementation is easy, requiring few resources and limited cost. The additional innovation is for dispensing drugs using a robot, which picks the medications and inserts them into the bottle specific to a prescription ordered by the physician. Then, a label is printed and applied, and the bottle is boxed and ready for shipment. The order is received via machine-to-machine. Humans perform only the quality check.

Some would argue that Level 3 and 4 innovations are not true innovations; yet, it is not the organization that judges innovation, but rather the individual recipient. Satisfying a need, with better than expected performance, changes purchasing behaviors and attitudes (long-term) about satisfaction.

Global Targeting, Inc. designs for success by achieving the ultimate outcome, not by meeting someone's definition of innovation. Level 3 and 4 ideas can succeed and be truly innovative. Level 3 and 4 innovations accomplish this task but without the fanfare, receiving little attention and often insignificant management support.

Innovation efforts quickly die due to the lack of support from management, team, or customer (patient). The apps developed for patient monitoring and self-monitoring of health status or chronic conditions did not come from traditional sources. Self-monitoring apps and devices were developed by the fitness industry. Physicians developed apps that they provide to the patients. The FDA (US Food & Drug Administration) did not decide to regulate medical and healthcare apps until 2011 and released guidelines in 2013 for review (Wicklund, 2013). In other words, this innovation happened outside the healthcare industry and was only later adopted for use.

Figure 4.2 lists seven reasons that kill innovation. Insufficient buy-in and lack of support are the key reasons for failure. In addition, motivational issues, lack of experience

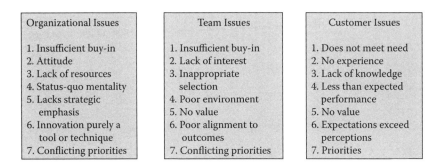

Organizational Issues	Team Issues	Customer Issues
1. Insufficient buy-in	1. Insufficient buy-in	1. Does not meet need
2. Attitude	2. Lack of interest	2. No experience
3. Lack of resources	3. Inappropriate selection	3. Lack of knowledge
4. Status-quo mentality	4. Poor environment	4. Less than expected performance
5. Lacks strategic emphasis	5. No value	5. No value
6. Innovation purely a tool or technique	6. Poor alignment to outcomes	6. Expectations exceed perceptions
7. Conflicting priorities	7. Conflicting priorities	7. Priorities

Figure 4.2   Seven reasons that kill innovation.

with the item, unachievable levels of performance, and poor alignment with the innovative outcome aid in failure.

Treating innovation as a technique (or application) assumes that present systems can handle the rigor required of innovation efforts. This assumption is synonymous with treating a disease without understanding its cause and origin. Innovation becomes more of an event than an established strategy and therefore occurs spontaneously, rather than systemically.

Concerted or focused management support requires dedicated individuals, a well-communicated and fully implemented management strategy, and sufficient resources. Otherwise, innovation occurs as a chance event. The most difficult aspect of innovation projects is that they are not daily projects or operations. They happen outside the daily work routines. When originality is required, management must step outside their comfort zone and be willing to break with tradition by allowing time and resources for innovation to occur. These types of innovation not only accentuate risk, but also involve increased rewards.

The goal is to sustain (continue) the gains made by the innovation. Sustained innovation is a result of a successful ENOVALE approach. Sustained innovation occurs when the customer or patient changes his or her behavior and adopts the new paradigm as the new normal. The performance they seek exceeds their expectations, and then they judge the result as innovative.

ENOVALE: A Key Strategy for Project Success

Before implementing the project, each idea/need pair must follow the ENOVALE Solutions process in order to become an innovative outcome bounded by its requirements, assumptions, and limitations. Consider the following example.

Background

Due to the use of smartphones and associated apps (applications), innovations in care happen daily and are transforming care delivery. Physiological monitoring transmits automatically to physicians and nurses who can immediately call or send a message to the patient to discuss why their vital signs or symptoms are changing, such as if their blood sugar level is out of control or moving in the wrong direction. Care managers help patients keep their diabetes, hypertension, and medication levels under control using this function. These patients can stay home and attend to their normal activities. At the same time, the monitoring allows corrections before untoward events happen.

Integration of data from medical devices to the electronic medical record was a $3.5 billion business in 2013 and is projected to grow to $33.5 billion in 2018 with a 37.8% growth per year (Millard, 2013). In addition to the automatic alerts for providers and caregivers, this integration also engages patients to self-monitor and makes changes to their own lifestyle and health. This innovation occurs at the junction of medical devices and electronic medical records using the patient, physician, and caregiver in alignment with the smart devices.

Objective: Develop the application and verify its efficacy. Now, the process begins by determining viability, prior to developing the application. Consider the following questions and statements:

1. Is the objective valid and doable? (Use SMART criteria [**S**pecific, **M**easurable, **A**ttainable, **R**elevant, **T**imely].)
2. List the requirements (both user and functional; see Table 4.1). Define the parameters of efficacy.

Table 4.1 Functional/User Requirements

Items	User 1—Stent Application	User 2—Patient Reactions
Functional Requirement 1	Size, dimensional aspects	Reduces rehabilitation time
Functional Requirement 2	Meets proper strength requirements	Simpler technique
Functional Requirement 3	Is properly placed and oriented	Less anesthesia
Functional Requirement 4	No breakage or fracture	High effectiveness of procedure
Functional Requirement 5	Training for doctor/ staff minimal	Less complications
Functional Requirement 6	Meets quality standards	

3. Determine the assumptions (regarding performance, sales forecast, accuracy, reliability, etc.):
   a. Typical assumptions:
      i. Patient comfort with devices
      ii. Operational at least 99% of the time
      iii. Patient can use technology
      iv. 99%+ diagnosis accuracy
4. Determine the limitations (cost, risk, ease of use, etc.). Are these criteria restrictive or intransient?
   a. Typical limitations:
      i. Less technically savvy patients may deliberatively avoid
      ii. Requires good to excellent patient management
      iii. Have alternatives when technology fails
      iv. May not work as well in rural areas

Table 4.2 Risk-to-Success Scale: Medical Tracking App

Success	Risk	Quadrants	Number
15,000 units	Aversion to technology	Weakness	1
15,000 units	Impersonal approach	Weakness	2
15,000 units	Daily fluctuations	Weakness	3
50,000+ units	Does not extend quality of life	Strength	1
50,000+ units	Technological problems	Strength	2
35,000 units	Patients does not experience benefit	Status quo	1
35,000 units	Limited comfort factor	Status quo	2
35,000 units	Inconsistent use	Portal	1

5. Assess the success-to-risk ratio (use the SREM (Software Requirements Engineering Methodology) tool; see Table 4.2). Does risk outperform success?

Assessment of the success-to-risk factor requires an understanding of the proposed product. Table 4.2 describes a typical session where success and risk are balanced. At this stage, the success factor is only an estimate of expected benefit. Risk relates to underperformance. Risks include consequences and also alternatives. For a typical product, service, or technology, there are numerous benefits and risks. The precision and accuracy of this estimate are limited at this stage, but the information provides a catalyst for evaluation and decision making. The overall intent is to minimize the effects of risk in the final product. Information from Table 4.2 is transferred to Figure 4.3 for a visual interpretation. Too few strengths or too many weaknesses can stop a project immediately, whereas performance rated at "Status quo" may never achieve innovation

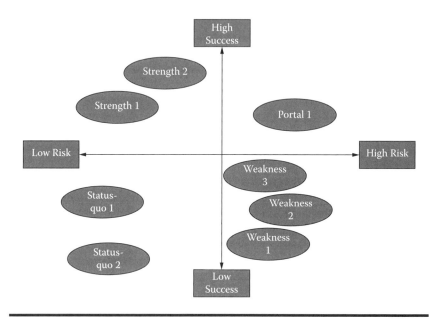

Figure 4.3 Application of the SREM tool. (From McLaughlin, G. and Caraballo, V., *Chance or Choice: Unlocking Innovation Success,* **Taylor & Francis, Boca Raton, FL, 2013.)**

status. Portals (opportunities) could be future revisions or future innovation projects.

Identify the innovative outcome (must pass steps 1 through 5). The innovative outcome would be an operational application (small scale) within 6 months. Should requirements, assumptions, or limitations be too rigid or incapable of performing, then management might decide to scrap this project, before committing further resources or capital. If it is acceptable, it goes on for further validation and financial evaluation.

Each means or type of innovation requires a slightly different process. Many elements share a common set of features and requirements. The true differentiator is the amount of originality. This governs confidentiality, security, and secrecy issues. Although some standardization is possible, innovation projects require a different set of strategies and a different process to be successful (Figure 4.4). A sufficient description of each step facilitates an understanding of how the process

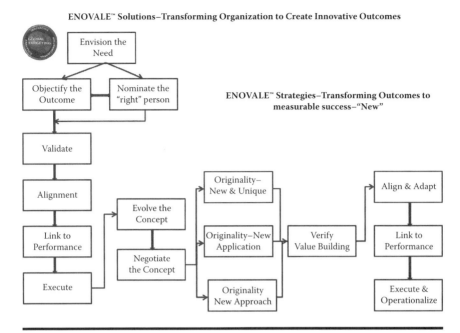

Figure 4.4 ENOVALE process for items classified as "new." (From Global Targeting, Inc., Chicago, IL. With permission.)

varies for each originality level. The assumption is that the project passed the ENOVALE Solutions seven-step process. The innovative outcome is valid, and the total cost to implement is acceptable. For illustration purposes, the innovation example described previously serves as an example to discuss each step of the ENOVALE Solutions seven-step process. The originality level (Level 2 for this item) implies that certain security and confidentiality arrangements are executed before approving the initial concept. In addition, management commitment, resource allocation, and sufficient capital must be present.

Step 1: Evolve the Concept

For Levels 1 and especially 2, idea/need pairs require a certain evolution of thought and application. Evolving the concept involves moving from innovative outcome to conceptualization. For the medical app described previously, the first step is to create a first-stage concept. This stage requires ideation (idea generation), a functioning team, available resources and technology, committed management, technical support, and dedicated support. The first-stage concept is similar to completing patent requirements—preparing initial drawings. There is a tangible, visible drawing and/or written process (for intangibles). Checking this information with the requirements established previously validates the continued efficacy of the project.

Levels 3 and 4 require less evolution and more understanding of the consequences. With these levels, the concept can go directly to paper, a layout, a map, or a set of sequential steps. Flowcharts are one method of documenting the concept as the tool consists of inputs, process steps, and outputs.

Step 2: Negotiate the Concept

For Levels 1 and 2, negotiation continues as the item changes and modifies. Parties (management, technical, and financial) negotiate from a position of equality. Management includes ancillary functions (sales/marketing, patient relations, HR, etc.) as needed. The objective guides the negotiation process. It is natural that some conflict or disagreement exists, thus permitting reassessment and reevaluation. Negotiations result in an evaluation of risk and rewards. Examining and ranking alternatives provides a "test of reality" and overall performance potential. At this time, negotiations occur using empirical evidence, experience, and common sense. The use of simulations is an excellent tool. Simulating various situations, problems, and operational concerns provides valuable information. Achievement of consensus provides the team with purpose, the capability to work through difficult situations, and the ability to make an informed decision as to whether to proceed or stop.

For the example project, concerns would revolve around usability, frequency, cost, validity of symptoms, etc., all of which require negotiation. Given that, the basic concept is complete, concerns such as alternatives, risks, and functionality can be fully negotiated and agreed upon. This stage or step moves from "idea" to "reality," with an additional opportunity to review, evaluate, and approve.

Step 3: Originality

Depending on the level of originality, this stage of the process can be different. For Levels 1 and 2, additional research into technology, legal, potential customer purchasing behavior, and other factors is critical. This process leads to a new definition of the product, service, or technology. Evaluation of the "new" item for its potential and overall benefits (financial, competitive, use, and life cycle) provides a natural accept/reject point in the project. A tangible prototype should be available for testing. For the Medical Diagnosis example, this stage takes the perspective of the users and their purchasing needs, wants, and expectations. A final definition of user performance regarding ease of use, significant time savings, accurate prognostication, and assessment of needs occurs.

For Levels 3 and 4, the step is simpler. Again, management and team members need further research into the item (perceptions and attitudes of prospective buyers, brand comparison, potential life cycle, ability to duplicate, etc.). At this point, rather than originality, the uniqueness (including its requirements/specifications, which are clearly specified) of the item is critical. The research provides another "checkpoint" for acceptance or rejection. Levels 3 and 4 move quickly through this process, using the customer (user's) viewpoint or actual input as a judgment point. The emphasis that Global Targeting places on analytics is on the method of interpreting this voluminous customer/patient/user data. Without it, the team relies on their personal judgment and experience, which may mislead. Decisions about "new" products and services come from these sources and provide numerous opportunities for new applications and approaches.

Step 4: Verify

This step is critical for finalizing a decision regarding a possible innovative outcome. Verification begins with confirmation. If an innovative outcome passed all criteria, confirmation to implement occurs. Implementation time varies with the amount of originality: the more original an item is, the longer the time to implement. It may mean that a pilot test of a new service or delivery model occurs at this point.

After receiving confirmation, the team assesses the availability of resources, both personal and process. Verify for both value and benefit. Finally, the design is operational. For the proposed example, the team confirms the approved design/concept with the focus moving to operational and logistical concerns. Marketing and finance can begin the planning process to address customer/patient/user needs.

Step 5: Align and Adapt

Team inconsistency (and management failure to support) occurs when the purpose or objective is not clearly understood or reviewed. To measure alignment of values, management distributes a survey to all team members. Knowing what team members expect and perceive predicts alignment to the objective. Supplementing this survey is a review of reality—is the outcome viable, doable? Is it truly innovative? Team member alignment promotes team advocacy that supports the project objective. Management must provide direct and unequivocal support; otherwise, conflicts and disruptions become daily (weekly) outcomes. Failure to offer this support diminishes the chances of success. Leadership must reinforce its commitment at this stage or face disruptions, delays, and excuses. This requires monitoring the existing environment— an assessment and realistic evaluation of benefit and overall potential. If conditions change, this warrants a modification to the strategy and an adjustment to the objective and innovative outcome.

For the example and all prospective projects, five key truths must remain consistent:

1. The objective remains consistent.
2. Ensure that all can support the objective.
3. The objective is valued.
4. Expectations remain positive.
5. Leadership remains fully committed.

By maintaining control of the objective, there is less drift or micro-modification. For example, some would want to include additional features to the software, consider eliminating personnel, and use the results exclusively for diagnosis. Even viable suggestions could cause further delays, team and member disagreements, confusion, and a distraction from the objective. Keeping the focus on the objective eliminates both human and processing problems.

Step 6: Link to Performance

A simplified step given the number of tracking measures are in progress. Each of the "new" types requires a different set of measures. The most common measures will be project and financial metrics. The key lies in defining the performance for each innovation type and then tracking these measures throughout the life of the project. Measures should also include human and process indicators. Long-term financial indicators or projections provide little information in the early decision-making stages, especially for Level 1 and 2 designs. Creating short-term indicators provides real-time information on various aspects of the innovation project. Creativity is important, as measures should involve at least two of the five senses and one or more perceptual evaluations. What we hear and see, feel, and believe

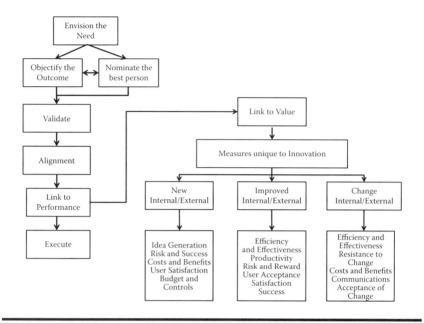

Figure 4.5   Link to performance and value for "new" innovation projects.

all contribute to the overall assessment of any project. Figure 4.5 details various measures for each "new" project theme.

For the Medical Diagnosis example, key sensory measures such as the look, feel, and voice characterization are critical. Perceptions/attitudes of patients are critical. These are "make-or-break" project measures. Obtain patient and staff reactions and comments with the use of focus groups or, to a lesser degree, focused surveys; during focus groups, trust leading versus lagging indicators for evaluative purposes. Be creative; with time and practice, this will become as natural as using standard measures.

Step 7: Execute

The final stage is one where design and development "hands off" to operations. Involve operations personnel early in the design process. Transfer knowledge, performance, and experiential data to operations to drastically reduce implementation time. To know if success is ensured, just examine the number of "surprise" issues. A well-evaluated and well-planned project should encounter few issues when entering the operations phase. Do provide the team with all significant learnings, as future applications and approaches will require significantly less time to complete.

For the example, the execution phase involves the final programming, acquiring the electronics/database, and finalizing the patient-facing interface. Simulation is an excellent tool for evaluation during the entire ENOVALE Strategies portion. A short cycle time in these last two phases (stages) enables testing and review. Actual implementation should begin during this final phase. Again, the frequency of issues is an excellent evaluator of success.

Summary

Depending on the originality of the design, "new" types of innovations are possible in the product, service, and technological areas of healthcare. Due to such items as smartphones and associated applications, innovations in care happen daily and are transforming care. Physiological monitoring transmits automatically to physicians and nurses, who can immediately call a patient to discuss why their vital signs are changing, for example, if their blood sugar level is out of control or moving in the wrong direction. Care managers help patients keep their diabetes, hypertension, and medication levels under control. These patients can stay home and attend to their normal activities. At the same, the monitoring allows corrections before untoward events occur. Originality is a key for these types of innovation.

Approving the innovative outcome justifies the project to commence. The ENOVALE Strategies for "new" projects guide the project team to success, given that the need and idea remain viable. The thoroughness of the ENOVALE methodology ensures that if success is justifiable, it will be verified.

With the end goal, competitive advantage, and customer (patient) satisfaction, the innovation introduced must meet an unsatisfied need with better than expected performance.

   This chapter presented a methodology for conducting a "new" themed innovation in healthcare. Applications were presented in the product, services, and to a lesser extent technological sectors of the healthcare space. Diversity is the best characteristic to describe "new" themed innovations combined with aspects of originality. Although this chapter did not provide a detailed explanation of each step in the ENOVALE process, it should have generated interest in pursuing this approach. Given that innovation begins and ends with the individual, the opportunities to create "new" themed innovation in the service sector provides solid reasoning for applying Innovation Process Management.

Discussion Questions

1. Given the fact that most people view innovation as a totally new product or service and that the most prevalent innovations are actually changing the way care is delivered, what can be done to foster Levels 2, 3, and 4 innovation?
2. After reviewing the steps defined in the ENOVALE process, which step or steps do you think would create the most resistance in your current work setting?

Assignments

1. Review your most recent patient or physician satisfaction data and pick one to use with the ENOVALE process. Identify the issue, and what need or want to address. Illustrate the issue and formulate the action using the ENOVALE steps.

2. How would you ensure that a Level 2 innovation could be sustained over time? What about a Level 3 innovation?

3. Develop at least one unsatisfied need. Begin with the need, and apply the criteria of sustainability, capability, and viability. Do you believe that the need could become an innovative outcome?

Chapter 5

Improvement Can Be Innovative!

Introduction

Understanding the concept of innovation requires both knowledge of what exists and what needs to exist. Unsatisfied (at times referred to as unclassified) needs, wants, or desires drive innovation. However, innovation thrives beyond inventions and new scientific breakthroughs. Innovation exists in the minds of those who evaluate and identify it. Individuals do not use a standard definition when deciding whether the encounter is innovative. Customers (patients/physicians) know innovation because of performance issues that exceed their expectations. To be told a product, service, or even technology is innovative is ludicrous. How can a marketer, salesperson, or spokesperson decide for every individual that something is innovative? Innovation is determined at the individual level. Individuals can experience an item, evaluate service, and determine if it meets an unfulfilled need—only then is it deemed innovative.

Implementation of an electronic medical record (EMR) is a good example of improving a process. With a paper chart, only one person can use the chart at a time. Many disciplines provide care to a hospitalized patient and often need to chart or review the record at the same time. Each admission for outpatient or inpatient service started historically with a new paper chart, and the old chart (history) was only delivered if requested. Electronic medical records contain the longitudinal history (old and new specific to the organization that owns the chart) along with current diagnosis and treatment. The real-time power of the information is truly innovative; it meets an unsatisfied need with better-than-expected performance.

Improvements can also occur incrementally. For example, with electronic records, several individuals can use the electronic chart at the same time. They might not even be in the same organization and often not in the same location. Coordination of care occurs through the linking of processes and communication among providers and caregivers. When implementing an electronic record, the team starts by mapping processes as they are at the time. Next, they look at workflows and possible changes that could enhance the workflow after adoption of the EMR. Workflow improvements are operational in nature and not innovative, yet the benefit is real.

Innovation born from improvement is the purpose of this chapter. Improvement contains all the characteristics of a new or original innovation. It meets unfulfilled needs (wants or desires), exceeds expectations of performance, and changes purchase behaviors (satisfies customers). The omission of any of the criteria would result in an improvement that may not be considered innovative.

Innovation as Improvement

For improvement to occur, there must be an original or existing item (product, technology, or service). Individuals will compare an existing item with an "improved" version by

1. Experience and knowledge of the item—the more experience an individual has with an item, the greater that improvement must be judged as innovative.
2. Examining its performance—performance refers to the tangible (and intangible) elements that define the product, technology, or service. Consider implementing a new policy to decrease wait times for operative procedures. Performance is the actual wait time; innovation is when significant improvement in the wait time occurs.
3. Determining whether it meets a new or unfulfilled need—innovation requires that improvement meets or replaces an existing need.

Improvement of an item may result in significant gains in market share and profits, but this gain is not innovation. Innovation goes beyond improvement as it sets a new level of expectations in how an item performs.

The value of examining the Innovation Model (Chapter 2, Figure 2.4) comes from those elements that relate directly to innovation assessment. Figure 5.1 is a portion of the

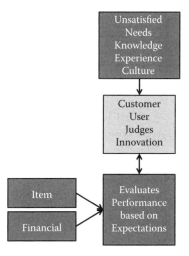

Figure 5.1   Excerpt from Innovation Model. (Adapted from McLaughlin, G. and Caraballo, V., *ENOVALE: How to Unlock Sustained Innovation Project Success,* Taylor & Francis, Boca Raton, FL, 2013.)

Innovation Model involved with the individual's decision process to judge innovation. Although cultural differences may influence the perceptions of innovation, research has demonstrated that when a need is satisfied and performance is better than expected, innovation is often recognized.

Judgment of innovation improvement requires experience with a product, technology, or service, as well as knowledge of the item itself. Judgment occurs when assessing performance. Performance measures an item's ability to accomplish its stated objective or purpose. Individuals compare what they expect against how the item performs. Therefore, a blanket's tangible performance is to keep in body heat while its intangible performance is to match the feel, color, style, and décor desired. Items can perform outside their stated objectives as well, thereby increasing the perception of improved performance.

Intangible items have no measureable aspect of performance (no physical measures). Yet, individuals judge when an item exceeds their expectations. This assessment corresponds directly to the innovation concept of performance. For example, patients can easily judge intangible aspects of a hospital stay and apply their experiences in other services to rating or ranking the organization. Patient satisfaction is perceptual and a critical measure of performance—individuals judge intangible items by comparing (contrasting) perceptions of performance with their own expectations. When expectations exceed perceptions, there is the possibility of recognized innovation.

Recognizing Innovation

Recognition of innovation when performance exceeds expectations (which meets some form of need) challenges the status quo. As mentioned previously, improvement is synonymous with techniques (strategies) such as Six Sigma, which improve

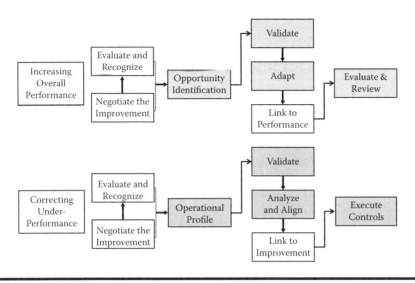

Figure 5.2   Improvement project ENOVALE™. (Adapted from McLaughlin, G. and Caraballo, V., *ENOVALE: How to Unlock Sustained Innovation Project Success,* **Taylor & Francis, Boca Raton, FL, 2013.)**

processes by reducing or eliminating defects (errors, mistakes, nonconformities, reportable incidences, etc.). This improvement is an admirable goal, requiring an understanding of the existing process. Continuous quality improvement must be a "best practice" for any organization. However, innovation moves beyond the control of defects to improving performance to exceed expectations. Although improving performance can lead to innovation, correcting underperformance (if it is chronic) can also be innovative. Here the division between techniques such as Six Sigma and Lean blur. Acknowledgment of innovation requires a drastic improvement in performance along with fulfilling a need. Shaded portions in Figure 5.2 indicate modified steps between the two outcomes.

Detailed information on implementing these steps is found in *ENOVALE: How to Unlock Sustained Innovation Project Success* (McLaughlin and Caraballo, 2013b).

Numerous measures comprise improvement opportunities. Of course, each could be improved (or returned to normal operations) with techniques such as Six Sigma/Lean. Improvement of measures will continue to meet customer (patient) expectations. Innovation moves beyond an expected return to that which satisfies a need by exceeding expectations.

An Example: Tangible Items

Assume patient recovery time is 4 weeks for knee replacement surgery; then introduction of an improved methodology that reduces the recovery time to 2 weeks is truly innovative. During the ENOVALE™ Solutions process, the team would evaluate recovery time as a viable innovation opportunity and classify which innovation type (New, Improve, or Change) is the best choice for implementing this opportunity. Without getting into specifics, detailed in Chapter 4, the team would evaluate the following:

1. The objective ... recovery time will be decreased by ...
2. Requirements ... both performance (functional) and patient related
3. Assumptions involved
4. Limitations involved
5. Cost-benefit analysis
6. Success-to-risk ratio

The team and management evaluate project efficacy, decide to fund, and execute. Normally, this exercise may take 4 to 6 hours (cost-benefit analysis time not included), with experience. Following up on the minimally invasive total knee surgery, a group comprised of the orthopedic surgeon, staff from the OR, physical therapy, and surgical nursing would meet to evaluate the differences in performing the minimally invasive total knee surgery and providing the post-op care.

They would evaluate costs of surgery, including any new equipment necessary to perform the surgery, along with the recovery requirements versus the expected reimbursement. They would identify the likely patient candidates along with any changes required in the OR, surgical nursing, and physical therapy.

Intangibles, although not often as easy to measure, are part of the innovation evaluation. Perceptions of patient satisfaction, attitude, behavior, and beliefs all constitute viable indicators of performance. These intangibles often dominate the criteria individuals use to judge innovation. Intangible items are estimated from tools such as surveys, focus groups, or interviews. These provide perceptual information that is often unstable in the short term. For example, the information about these perceptions comes from qualitative statements included with Likert scale surveys. They often include wait times, response times, cleanliness, ambiance, and staff attitudes.

An Example: Intangible Measures

Suppose a pharmaceutical company requires information from its customers to assess one aspect of performance, namely brand recognition. The organization decides to use a focus group, presenting them with similar products to evaluate and rank. The organization wants to know how well potential customers will recognize the product name, its manufacturer (distributor), and similar competitive products. The measure of performance is the perception of "recognition." This recognition is an intangible because it would vary from one individual to the next. Using a survey, during the focus-group process, the company could measure the degree and importance of recognition. The outcome is to improve recognition so that the organization's products could be viewed as innovative. Informing customers (patients) about an innovative product or service requires previous knowledge and experience with the product or service. When dealing with intangibles, remember that people use their five senses to evaluate the product, technology, or service. That is why patients often comment on cleanliness, ambiance, and staff response time. They comment on how they are treated, who recognizes their need, and finally who responds to it.

Choose ENOVALE Strategies (Figure 5.2) when

1. Performance and expectations exceed what presently exists.
2. Inconsistent performance below expectations or when improving performance would be recognized as innovative.

When performance meets expectations (status quo), then invest in Six Sigma/Lean (or another continuous quality improvement initiative) to initiate incremental improvements.

Performance and Innovation

Identifying how an item performs and then recognizing an improvement in that performance is how individuals recognize innovation. Therefore, a need exists to define and measure performance in various healthcare sectors. Defining performance requires both a standard from which to judge an item and an understanding of the purpose (or reason) for the item. An item's performance must have a history, one that is familiar to the individual. A person cannot judge wait time at a doctor's office until he or she has experienced such an event. Often when experience is not available, people set expectations based on some similar encounter. Whatever the case, individuals establish expectations and then judge performance based on those experiences. With a unique and original innovation where experience does not exist, the individual will use new information or compare performance to a similar item.

Performance must be measured and compared to a standard to determine whether the performance changed.

Performance can be as simple as the time expended to do a task or as complicated as satisfying an unhappy customer (patient). Performance, then, requires a mechanism to measure completion or fulfillment of an item's purpose. Measurement instruments can vary from the mechanical/electronic to beliefs and attitudes. The continuum is wide and varied. For measurement,

1. Use creative idea processes to develop and test new forms of measurement.
2. Begin with simple measures that require little explanation. For example, just examining the facial expressions of patients, using the new diagnostic system previously discussed, would provide a great indication of satisfaction and justification.

Two essential qualities of a measurement are that the measure is both valid (accurate) and reliable (repeatable). Prescribed methods for testing these variables exist, but a simpler commonsense approach is to identify each time the measure predicts correctly. Do not be concerned with "exacts" rather than noticeable variations. Measurements are not perfect but they do serve the purpose of informing when a change is underway.

Measurements require a set of standards from which to judge performance. If the standards are validated, then small changes in performance can be easily detected. Given that innovation judgment begins with the individual, feelings, perceptions, attitudes, and beliefs are critical. More often than not, these measures occur partially or not at all. Yet performance is judged by experience. To gather this information, most marketing/research professionals use focus groups, surveys, and interviews. This information may seem less than scientific but without an understanding of how an individual defines innovation, it is impossible. The user's perspective is critical—especially as it applies to experience and performance. Knowledge about what a customer or patient truly needs (and wants) is the key to purchasing behaviors and patient satisfaction. Unfortunately, this information is only possible at the time the product or service is used or rendered. Asking individuals to fill out surveys "after the fact" is often useless or, worse, incorrect. Satisfaction is a short-term phenomenon—perspectives change greatly with time. With real-time information systems available (cell/smartphones, Internet connectivity, face-to-face contact), this critical information must be part of an innovation management process. Once a competitor gains this knowledge, their business (or yours) will never be the same. One method to better understand these measures is to think about the tangible and intangible aspects of any product, service, or technological evaluation.

Depending on the sector, performance measures include both tangible and intangible aspects. Tangibles items in a hospital setting, for example, could include

1. Patient recovery time, length-of-stay, response time, etc.
2. Resource allocation, staff-to-patient ratios, utilization, etc.
3. Employee efficiency, costs, expenses, etc.

Numerous measures comprise improvement opportunities. Of course, each could be improved (or returned to normal operations) with techniques such as Six Sigma/Lean. Improvement of measures will continue to meet customer (patient) expectations. Innovation moves beyond an expected return to that which satisfies a need by exceeding expectations.

Services, products, or technology can underperform, perform as expected, or overperform. Patients, customers, or user expectations can be satisfied, unsatisfied, or judged better than expected. Performance can be below requirements, meet requirements, or exceed requirements. If performance is below its requirements (potential), then an innovation management project may be warranted.

ENOVALE Strategies

Figure 5.2 details the steps for the improvement phase. Similar to information described in Chapter 4, Step 1 is both recognition of the problem/opportunity and evaluation of performance. Evaluating performance requires a baseline (built upon a set standard). Creation of a baseline requires four unique elements (McLaughlin and Caraballo, 2013b):

1. Identification of a metric that best measures performance
2. Identification of a proper measuring instrument or device
3. Creation of an appropriate scale to rate the performance
4. Consistent, accurate, and timely observations

Elements 1, 2, and 4 were discussed previously. Element 3 requires an understanding of maximum and minimum operating ranges, safety, and risk. A scale must include a range of values, settings, or graduated increments. The scale should be centered on the most common or expected response, and encompass a range of values including extreme values, collection of data that is numerical or convertible to numerical. This type of data is simpler to analyze. Next, the data is examined for chronic incidences that can affect performance stability.

As part of the evaluation step, identify performance achievement or success. Where in the scale does performance go from expected to exceeding expectations? This point signifies the criteria for success. Conversely, where does failure occur? Both success and failure require that a set of instructions (or process) is available to reduce the incidence of failure and increase the occurrence of success.

Negotiating the improvement (Step 2) revisits team membership and any issues that remain. The initial team that created the innovative outcome may not be best for project work. Those individuals who best recognize innovation as improvement will make the best choice. Consider how the project affects staff, process, or resources. New team members often bring energy and enthusiasm to the project. Negotiate a project schedule, milestones, and responsibilities. Use this step to examine, in more detail, the cost/benefit ratio. Continue negotiating until agreement to proceed is unanimous. The project is ready for implementation. Performance either needs improvement or requires a boost in performance to stay competitive.

Overperformance and Innovation

There are times when an item must perform above its stated expectations to be considered innovative. Incrementally increasing improvement may be of great benefit but not innovative. Techniques such as Lean Six Sigma provide the mechanism to achieve incremental performance. However, when performance significantly improves by fulfilling new needs, innovation is present (whether fully recognized or not). A business or organization would need to innovate when faced with strong competitive issues. This driving force could result in significant performance enhancement that creates a distinctive competitive performance.

Step 3: Identify Opportunities

Figure 5.2 details the steps for improvement when the objective is to exceed existing performance. The third step is to identify opportunities for improvement. Operating from a baseline, determine which element(s) could perform better, and determine its (their) requirements and whether it (they) can be improved incrementally or with additional investment (resources, personnel, materials). Finally, establish a realistic improvement goal (e.g., performance needs to increase x% to achieve a competitive advantage). Sustained improvement is the objective.

An increase in performance assumes that existing performance is consistent and meeting requirements. To improve performance, select those aspects or parts of the process capable of supporting radical improvement. By improving these components (elements), the entire unit performance will increase. The key is to begin with a consistent process, as inconsistencies require incremental improvement. Begin by examining the "process" (operation, activity) that generates the outcome. Which elements can improve or out-perform past results? Select the elements, test these at the new performance levels, and examine the results. If the outcome is greatly improved, there is success! Now, does this improved performance meet additional or unfulfilled needs? If it does, then the improvement may be innovative.

Step 4: Validate

Validate the choice through various means. Examine data, if possible, to determine which elements must change to exceed performance expectations. Another way is to use the power of human experience to evaluate the effect of improving an element and its resulting influence on the process in general. One such tool is the Success Modes and Performance Analysis (SMPA) diagram (see Figure 5.3). The SMPA analysis evaluates components or elements that increase performance and sustain that performance over time (McLaughlin and Caraballo, 2013b). The tool focuses on the positive influences of improving performance beyond present expectations. Identification of an element to improve requires additional evaluation, a new set of standards/baseline measures, and a new goal to achieve.

Consider the following example: Say a patient complaint is about excessive wait times before entering the surgical unit. Most organizations start with a root cause analysis. They look

Process Step	Key Process Input	Potential Success Modes	Potential Performance	PRB	Potential Causes	NEP	Current Actions or Controls	SUS	SPN	Actions Recommended
What is the process step?	What is the component, part or element?	In what ways can the component, part, or element improve?	What is the effect on performance?	Impact Probability—Rate the chance of continued improvement	What could cause the component, part, or element to affect performance negatively?	How frequently would a negative effect occur?	What actions (controls) are needed for this improvement to be sustained?	How well can the improvement sustain increased performance?	Success Priority Number	What are the actions required for maintaining improved performance?
	Customer's available time	Less wait time	Judged more efficient	10	Problems with routing	6	Modify software	5	300	
	Customer's available time	Less wait time	Judged more efficient	10	Problems with routing	6	Increase operators	1	60	
	Customer's available time	Less wait time	Judged more efficient	10	Problems with routing	6	Increase menu options	10	600	Check feasibility of increased menu selection
	Customer's available time	Less wait time	Judged more efficient	10	Software	8	Purchase or design software	8	640	Check available hardware for purchase
	Customer's available time	Less wait time	Judged more efficient	10	Human interaction	8	Training, follow-up	6	480	

Process or Product Name: — Improve Wait Time — Prepared by: — Page ___ of ___

Team: — SMPA Date (Orig) ___ (Rev) ___

Figure 5.3 SMPA example worksheet. (Adapted from McLaughlin, G. and Caraballo, V., *ENOVALE: How to Unlock Sustained Innovation Project Success*, Taylor & Francis, Boca Raton, FL, 2013.)

to see where the patient was delayed, in admitting, testing, or the Emergency Department. Next, they review the causes of the delays in these departments or in transporting the patient from one area to another. They evaluate admission orders because a patient requires a physician order for admission. Process improvement focuses on improvement in each of the areas just described. Innovation could take the form of bedside admitting. The patient presents with an order or the physician calls in an admission order. When the patient arrives, he may be immediately transported to the assigned room. Bedside admission and testing occur without the need to transport the patient to the lab. Instead, the phlebotomist extracts the blood from the patient at the bedside. The wait time is reduced and the process is fully revamped.

Step 5: Adaptation

Implementation of changes that affect existing performance goals and expectations require strong leadership and management support. Adaptation is a business-wide activity to communicate and align the business to the new standards of performance. The proposed modifications may require input from other sources, and therefore a process of consensus may follow. After initiating the adaptation process, further improvements should be simpler to implement. Performance enhancements require user approval about who will either judge the improvement innovative or not. Adaptation is then both an internal and external process.

Underperformance and Innovation

Step 3: Operational Profile

Underperformance is either an opportunity or a problem-solving event. Whatever the approach, it requires an understanding of the reasons and causes for the less-than-expected performance. Remember that performance is what the customer/patient/user experiences, so information (data) from this source is essential. Once identified, the less-than-expected performance must have one or more elements that are causing this phenomenon. This step begins the process of identifying these elements, determining their criticality, and assessing the effect on operations.

Some common but effective tools include the use of brainstorming to frame the problem; cause-and-effect diagrams to examine its effect; and a cause-and-effect matrix (Figure 5.4) when the cause of the underperformance is convoluted or multi-sourced. The purpose of this step is to observe and confirm the instances of underperformance.

Step 4: Validate

Validation's emphasis is on data collection and analysis. Identification of the causes and reasons for the underperformance provide criteria for remedying the problem. By applying the appropriate "fix," process monitoring can confirm whether the change in performance is permanent or transient. Key concerns are predictability, influence of lesser effects on performance, and the need for sufficient control plans. One excellent method of defining failure points is the use of the FMEA (failure modes and effect analysis).

The FMEA (Figure 5.5) is helpful in preventing future problems. It uses the power of human experience and judgment to facilitate a process of evaluating underperformance to prevent its recurrence and harmful effects.

Step 5: Analyze and Align

Data plays a key role in this phase. Interpretation of the data is critical to analysis. The team wants to ensure that the elements affecting performance do so regularly, and that the effect is

		Cause and Effect Matrix															
Rating of Importance to Customer (needs) or Project Objective (requirements)		1	2	3	4	5	6	7	8	9	10	11	12	13	14	15	
Choose either a Cause or Process Step		Need/Requirement	Need/Requirement	Need/Requirement	Need/Requirement	Need/Requirement	Need/Requirement	Need/Requirement	Need/Requirement	Need/Requirement	Need/Requirement	Need/Requirement	Need/Requirement	Need/Requirement	Need/Requirement	Need/Requirement	Total
Process Step	**Cause**																
1																	0
2																	0
3																	0
4																	0
5																	0
6																	0
7																	0
8																	0
9																	0
10																	0
11																	0
12																	0
13																	0
14																	0
15																	0
16																	0
17																	0
18																	0
19																	0
20																	0
																	0
																	0
Total		0	0	0	0	0	0	0	0	0	0	0	0	0	0	0	

Figure 5.4 Cause-and-effect matrix. (Adapted from McLaughlin, G. and Caraballo, V., *ENOVALE: How to Unlock Sustained Innovation Project Success*, Taylor & Francis, Boca Raton, FL, 2013.)

Failure Modes and Effects Analysis
(FMEA) Note: Failure = loss of performance

Prepared by: _____

Page _____ of _____

FMEA Date (Orig) _____ (Rev) _____

Process or Product Name: _____

Responsible: _____

Process Step	Critical Element	Potential Failure Mode	Potential Failure Effects	SEV	Potential Causes	OCC	Current Controls	DET	RPN	EOC	Actions Recommended	Resp.	Actions Taken	SEV	OCC	DET	RPN
Identify process step (if needed)	What is the critical element or part?	In what ways can this go wrong (fail)?	What is the consequence on performance?	How severe is the failure effect to the project objective?	What causes the critical element or part to go wrong?	How often does a cause occur?	What are the existing controls and procedures (inspection and test) that prevent loss of performance?	How well can you detect the cause?			What are the actions for reducing the occurrence of the cause, or improving detection?	Who's responsible for the recommended action?	What are the actions taken with the recalculated RPN? **Be sure to include completion month/year**				
									0								0
									0								0
									0								0
									0								0
									0								0

Figure 5.5 FMEA. (Adapted from McLaughlin, G. and Caraballo, V., ENOVALE: How to Unlock Sustained Innovation Project Success, Taylor & Francis, Boca Raton, FL, 2013.)

similar in magnitude. Changes to the process will introduce the need for new or refined requirements. Improvements to performance must be more than incremental; these improvements need to generate interest in the product, service, or technology and be judged as innovative. Remember to accept a holistic view of the process rather than focus on a simple component of improvement.

Alignment concerns the team, customers (users), and the organization. Consensus must exist before recognition of any improvement. Alignment is complete when the innovation is understood as meeting a new set of standards, a new standard of success. Communication is fundamental to informing the user that the item now consistently meets his expectations. That is, the customer or patient is satisfied with the present process as he experiences the improvements. Alignment is "people-oriented," and it is successful when achieving consensus.

Step 6: Link to Performance/Improvement

Step 6 (Figure 5.6) is common to both performance states. This step begins with how the customer (patient) or user views innovation (i.e., how an individual experiences and perceives innovation derived from improvement). Either the customer will change his purchase patterns, given the perceived innovation, or the patient will express his satisfaction with the services or products provided. The value of this information is critical for determining future sales, revenues, costs, and benefits; because innovation is not without risk, the more a business or organization can predict, with accuracy, financial, efficiency, or human benefits, the more predictive the forecasts will become. The assumption is that a change in performance (coupled with meeting an unsatisfied need) will be innovative. One last point: any innovation should serve the needs of the organization as well as the patient (customer) or user.

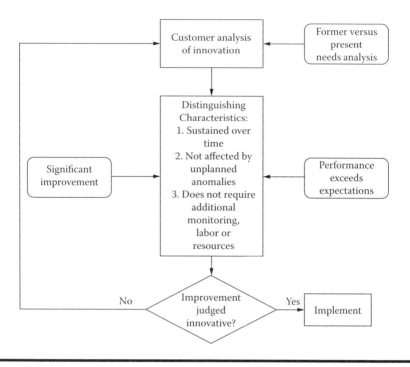

Figure 5.6 Link to performance/improvement step. (Adapted from McLaughlin, G. and Caraballo, V., *ENOVALE: How to Unlock Sustained Innovation Project Success,* Taylor & Francis, Boca Raton, FL, 2013.)

Step 7: Execute Controls

To maintain a new level of performance requires a set of controls (control plans, action items, and responsibilities). Sustaining performance levels requires applicable controls. Controls can be either procedural or automatic (e.g., alerts in CPOE, computerized physician order entry). After identifying a failure, the control plan should require a set of specific actions to occur along with those responsible for executing these actions. An excellent tool for controlling performance is the Control FMEA (Figure 5.7). This tool has applications outside traditional businesses with modification. Service businesses can use a similar tool by identifying operations where performance improvements recently occurred. By identifying

Failure Modes and Effects Analysis (FMEA) - Control Process

Innovation Team Project #		FMEA Date:	FMEA Revison #

Control Process

FMEA No.	Process Step	Improve Elements	Control Elements	Failure Modes	Severity	Potential Causes	Occurrence	Contin-gency Plans	Responsi-bilities	Remedial Action Plan	Detection	RPN	Audit Item
FMEA No. (Tracking only)	How is the Process Step being improved?	Which critical elements were selected for improvement?	What actions will be taken to control each improvement Element?	In what ways can the Control Element fail?	How severe is the Failure Mode to meeting project objectives?	What causes the Control Element to fail?	How often does the Cause occur?	What are the plans to prevent the Failure Mode or actions to take when failure occurs?	For each Failure Mode, list who, what, when, and how the remediation will occur	What are the checks and balances? (**Document the Remedial Action Plan**)	Will the checks and balances be able to detect non-compliance?	What is the Risk Priority Number?	Yes/No? (**A high RPN requires an Audit Plan**)
											0	
											0	
											0	
											0	

Figure 5.7 Control FMEA. (Adapted from McLaughlin, G. and Caraballo, V., ENOVALE: How to Unlock Sustained Innovation Project Success, Taylor & Francis, Boca Raton, FL, 2013.)

failure points (process, product, or human), a service business or organization can then identify potential failure modes (what the customer/patient/user experiences) and devise reasonable control/action plans. Control plans ensure predictability and consistency.

Consider the following example:

> Implementation of an electronic medical record (EMR) is a good example of improving a process. For years, performance varied under a variety of systems. With a paper chart, only one person could use the chart at time. Many disciplines provide care to a hospitalized patient and often need to chart or to review the record at the same time. Each admission for outpatient or inpatient service started with a new paper chart and the old chart (history) was only delivered if requested. Electronic medical records contain the longitudinal history along with current diagnosis and treatment. This is an improvement that vastly changed performance (speed, accuracy, and availability) of the records.
>
> Several individuals can use the EMR at the same time. Coordination of care occurs through the linking of processes and communication among providers and caregivers. When implementing an EMR, the team starts by mapping processes as they are at the time. Next, they look at workflows and possible changes that could enhance the workflow after adoption of the EMR. Process improvements occur internally; however, innovation may not, as the patient has had little interaction with his records. The fact that a better, accurate system was needed to protect and vastly reduce risks to patients was a given (objective). The EMR is an improvement because it fills a need and vastly increases performance.

Summary

Improvement is the simplest form of innovation to identify. Individuals have previous experience with the performance of an item; and when their expectations are exceeded (and an unsatisfied need met), *innovation* may be present. This is in contrast to *incremental improvement,* which "identifies and fixes" a problem with a process. Operationally, continuous or incremental improvement should be a fundamental strategy for all businesses.

To achieve innovation improvement, a specific strategy was discussed depending upon whether performance is below expectations or whether it must improve to stay competitive or meet more stringent customer needs, wants, or desires. This chapter included a discussion about when performance is rated below expectations and when it must exceed present expectations. For success, the improvement must be consistently evaluated, must perform without large deviations, and must be predictable over time.

Discussion Questions

1. Explain why performance is so critical for improvement. Pick an example of an innovation and describe how it outperforms its competition.
2. Are improved innovations the best choice application for the healthcare sector, considering time to implement, direct influence on the patient, simplest to identify?
3. Identify a product, service, or technology that is underperforming. How could improving the performance significantly be evaluated as innovative?
4. Identify four (4) patient-leading processes or techniques that, if they became innovative, would dramatically change the patient's perception of satisfaction.

Assignments

1. Choose a familiar process, item, or service that, if it out-performs, could be considered innovative. Prepare and use the SMPA diagram to answer this.

2. Select a critical process in your healthcare facility or business. Use the FMEA template to identify critical failure modes and its effect on performance.

3. Consider the process of distributing meals to patients. Identify at least one improvement that could significantly improve patient satisfaction and process efficiencies.

4. How would you measure an intangible quantity, such as patient contentment?

Chapter 6

Innovation from Proactive Change

Introduction

Can change in the healthcare space be innovative? The answer will challenge some, while others will agree wholeheartedly. Change is a process; it has an outcome; it is designed to meet one or more needs; individuals evaluate the change. How often have stories arisen about an individual who made a life-changing decision—one that affected that individual and others? The outcomes are positive, life changing, and meet one or more needs. The result of positive change can be innovative, or not. The determination of this status rests with the individual.

Can Change Be Innovative?

The answer is a resounding, yes! Organizations can experience the same euphoria when a decision leads to a positive outcome, given the fulfillment of one or more needs, wants, or desires. The definition of change, from an innovative perspective, is a decision made to replace something (a process, a procedure, a policy, etc.) with an appropriate (better) substitute.

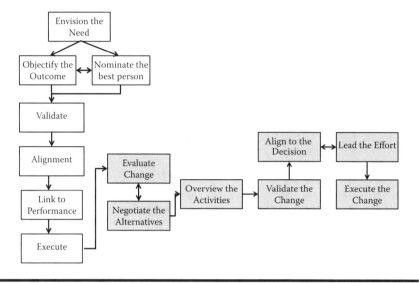

Figure 6.1 ENOVALE™ change strategies. (Adapted from McLaughlin, G. and Caraballo, V., *ENOVALE: How to Unlock Sustained Innovation Project Success,* Taylor & Francis, Boca Raton, FL, 2013.)

In healthcare, changing medications fits this definition. The need arises to change a medication due to a less-than-positive outcome. This need drives a decision: to both recognize the problem and initiate a decision. The decision makers (the doctors and pharmacists) use their experience and knowledge (see Figure 6.1) to identify appropriate criteria for selection. Their response will have a direct consequence on the patient. Finally, the decision creates a replacement medication with a new product or new dosage. The intent is to achieve a more positive outcome.

Change-related outcomes are either positive (and may be innovative), neutral, or negative. Some definitions apply:

- *Positive change:* results that have lasting value and significant improvement.
- *Neutral change:* results that have limited value and do not modify the status quo.
- *Negative change:* results that have negative value and deteriorate or worsen the present situation.

A positive outcome may not always have the desired end result. When this occurs, innovation is nonexistent. For this book, the consequences and repercussions of neutral or negative change are not of interest. One note: although the outcome is positive, the decision-making process must consider all consequences and repercussions for it to be innovative.

The most dramatic effects of change occur in individuals. Individuals experience change frequently and can judge its viability, effectiveness, and implementation. Given the frequency of change, it is no wonder that many fear change because of its negative connotations, even when change produces positive outcomes. When change yields a negative outcome, the lasting damage may be irreversible. Even neutral results (outcomes) may cause damage. Consider the use of disinfectants in hospitals. Since powerful disinfectants were banned, the number of deaths associated with the spread of disease has increased. The decision was a neutral outcome, yet the repercussions were devastating for some. The repercussions led to an innovation. The use of copper surfaces inhibits the growth of bacteria and viruses. Installation of ultraviolet lights was found to kill bacteria and viruses, and eliminate the need for some of the previously used disinfectants. However, a decision made without examining and evaluating the consequences and repercussions is foolish. However, decision making at the highest levels generally uses judgment and experience. While this combination works much of the time, for innovation it will lead to failure significantly more than 50%.

Unplanned or spontaneous change, usually associated with emergencies, can also yield neutral or negative consequences/ repercussions. Innovation is not a spontaneous event; it is planned and orchestrated. Ideation (generation of ideas) is spontaneous at times, and from this ideation the beginning elements of innovation occur. For the purposes of this book, planned change results in a positive outcome.

Planned change requires leadership, resources, and specific strategy. Leadership needs to accept the role of "orchestra leader," coaching, directing, and organizing. Planned change can easily produce an innovative or non-innovative solution. It depends on the requirements of the patients, customers, and users. If there is a distinctive advantage to change, then the appropriate approach is innovation.

Change can and does occur without being innovative. For some situations, it is more about the process of change than the actual change itself. Consider the closing of the US Army's Walter Reed Hospital. This change precipitated a neutral outcome, yet many were affected when the aged building closed its doors. Here, the intent was good (i.e., updating facilities) but the consequence was poor. For some, the results were negative and will have a time-dependent effect, …yet it was time to retire the facilities. When making decisions without fully examining the consequences, the outcome is often perceived in a neutral or negative manner. Closure of a facility is never 100% positive. However, the process of closing the facility while still meeting the needs of existing patients results in a more positive outcome. This outcome is why innovative change is often infrequent. Those who do embark on this process will have a distinct competitive advantage, as their outcomes will achieve results that are more positive.

The key is to understanding the nature of change: it begins with a decision (much like an idea or concept) and ends with an outcome. The ENOVALE™ methodology provides the means to evaluate the change from an innovative perspective. The development and execution of the decision is a process that can follow the ENOVALE method to yield a positive outcome. Figure 6.1 displays both ENOVALE Strategies. The Change strategies, seven elements, are highlighted in light gray.

Decision Making and Change

Decision making is pervasive in healthcare, where there is a need for innovative approaches and positive outcomes. So often, decisions come from an emotional or purely experiential perspective. Some are driven by need (response to disaster, trauma, etc.); some are driven by circumstance (cost, improving patient care, etc.); others for a specific purpose (expand facilities). Large changes result in the need for strategic decision making. In the pharmaceutical industry, RIF (Reduction in Force) is a constant and cyclical threat. Given the life cycles of products, there may be a need to reduce the workforce as a product loses patent protection. This constant threat is part of the culture but its effect is devastating. Decisions made to reduce the workforce done strategically are able to minimize negative effects. Decisions made without the benefit of even a simple process tend to cause more anxiety and affect overall productivity. These kinds of reductions often follow a prescription to cut staff by some percentage. No review of processes, needs, or consequences occurs with this methodology.

ENOVALE Change Strategies

Once the innovative outcome exits, the ENOVALE Solution phase and change is the preferred innovative approach, and the process presented in Figure 6.1 can begin. The first step is to evaluate the outcome in terms of making a change. The intent is not to improve, nor is there a focus on performance; rather, the need is for replacement.

Step 1: Evaluate the Change

Because the largest component of change is the process of making a decision, one must evaluate the change with this in mind. Issues such as leadership, advocacy, and good project management influence a successful outcome. Traditionally, most decisions begin at the executive level, in private, without the assistance of those directly affected by the change. This process works well for day-to-day decisions that do not require extensive evaluations, such as innovation; because most decisions are experience driven, resistance can be rampant. Evaluation is recommended to consider the consequences of a decision. For this reason, the first step begins with an additional evaluation of the proposed change.

What initiates change is one or more specific reasons. A simple but effective tool to evaluate the reasons for change is the "SNIFF" test (McLaughlin and Caraballo, 2013b). Consider the following six questions:

S Is the need for change simple or complex?
N Is there a new or recently exposed reason for the change, or is it simply a recycled idea?
I Could the change be judged as integrated (in conjunction with overall corporate goals) or reactionary?
F Is the reason for the change based on facts (evidence) rather than emotion?
F Will it be a final (permanent) change or one that is temporary?

If management and the team disagree on how each group would answer these questions, then reconsider the purpose or reason for the change. Also consider the human consequences of change that influence performance, attitude, and retention. Change affects people by

- Replacing, rearranging, or reassigning people
- Creating a new environment and causing readjustment
- Affecting more than basic needs; there are physical and emotional components
- Disrupting the status quo, bringing about a new order

Evaluation should not only be internal, but external as well. If you know how customers, patients, or users will react, a final decision maker can use this information wisely. When reviewing a prospective change, balance the risk and reward with the consequences of failure. Negative implications of change include, but are not limited to,

- Loss of productivity, support for organizational goals
- Increased costs, lost revenue from dissatisfied customers/patients/users
- Decreases in motivation and morale
- Need for emotional and psychological counseling
- Increase in employee resistance
- Increasing consequences of risk

Balance the positive with the negative when evaluating an innovation.

Step 2: Negotiate the Alternatives

Continuing the assessment of a pending change, this step reviews possible alternatives and consequences. Alternatives provide a mechanism for not only reviewing possibilities, but also examining the consequences of accepting or rejecting the alternative. An *alternative* could be anything from a different path, using a different resource/person, an added/deleted step, etc.—a choice. Do not confuse an alternative with a minor change, which is common. A change in an alternative always influences a consequence. A *consequence* is an outcome. For example, alternative procedures or medicines should produce a different outcome, if effective. For innovation purposes, alternative(s) change the outcome of the innovation to produce a negative, neutral, or positive effect.

An alternative must exhibit characteristics such as (McLaughlin and Caraballo, 2013b)

- Be 100% viable; no loss in productivity
- Achieve the same goal or meet an acceptable trade-off; benefits are similar

- Meet corporate objectives, values, and ethical practices; not cost prohibitive
- Cause the least amount of disruption to process, product, and personnel

Alternatives provide choices. When evaluating an alternative, consider the following characteristics: Longevity, Comprehensiveness, Effectiveness, Benefit, and Viability. Rank these characteristics on a scale from 1 to 5, with 1 being least able to meet the characteristic to 5 exceeding the characteristic that exists presently. Simulations are an excellent method of proposing and testing alternatives. Choose the best alternative even if it not ranked first. With few or no alternatives, the best choice is for replacement. A replacement may also generate a new set of alternatives. Teams should never belabor this step but use it to review possibilities.

Finally, select a team that can accomplish the objective. Hold the team responsible for the decisions; do not consider that only management will select the best choice. Trust is key, as someone who is trusted is also valued! For help in selecting the best team, consider the criteria detailed in *Chance or Choice: Unlocking Innovation Success* by McLaughlin and Caraballo (2013a).

Step 3: Overview the Activities

After considering alternatives and their consequences, the team needs to review any repercussions that may follow. A *repercussion* is the aftermath effect (resulting effect) on an individual or group of individuals (McLaughlin and Caraballo, 2013b). With repercussions comes risk. With risk, the chance of failure increases. The AREA (Alternative Repercussion Effects Analysis) (Figure 6.2) tool is an excellent method to evaluate alternative/repercussion pairs.

The AREA will assist greatly with identifying sources of alternatives, causes of repercussions, and the resultant

Alternative and Repercussion Effects Analysis
(AREA) Note: Failure = Effect of the
Repercussion

Prepared by: _____

Page _____ of _____

Process or Product Name: _____

Responsible: _____

FMEA Date (Orig) _____ (Rev) _____

Process Step	Alternative	Repercussion	Potential Failure Effects	SEV How Severe is the effect to the project outcome?	Potential Causes	OCC How often does a cause occur?	Current Controls	DET How well can you detect the cause?	RPN	EOC	Actions Recommended	Resp.	Actions Taken	SEV	OCC	DET	RPN
Identify Process Step (if needed)	What is the Alternative?	Identify the Repercussions (failure points)	What is the effect on the outcome?		What causes or reasons for this effect?		What are the existing controls and procedures that minimize the effect on the outcome?				What are the actions for reducing the occurrence of the cause, or improving detection?	Who's Responsible for the recommended action?	What are the actions taken with the recalculated RPN? **Be sure to include completion month/year**				
									0								0
									0								0
									0								0
									0								0
									0								0
									0								0

Figure 6.2   AREA template. (Adapted from McLaughlin, G. and Caraballo, V., *ENOVALE: How to Unlock Sustained Innovation Project Success*, Taylor & Francis, Boca Raton, FL, 2013.)

effects of repercussions. In addition, the AREA tool generates Control and Action plans. Focus on the quality of suggestions rather than quantity. Remember that all actions are inter-related, and that some causes affect numerous repercussion/alternative pairs. Use this tool to eliminate the negative side of change. In conjunction with this analysis, begin the change process by remediating the repercussions. Be specific with the changes and communicate these when possible across the entire organization. The next step is the final evaluation step before implementation.

Step 4: Validate

Most decisions occur quickly but lack a strategic component. Immediate decisions need expertise and experience, but carry great risk. The risk is that the decision required is outside the experience base of the individual (group) making the deci-sion. Risk involves both the decision maker and the receiver (the beneficiary of the change). This risk is one reason to consider both the consequences and repercussions of any change decision.

Risk

All decisions carry some risk. Items such as culture, industry, and experience affect how risk is determined. For health-care as an industry, risk is a serious concern, given the life-and-death decisions and consequences that occur every day. Yet, the decision-making process often lacks review or even assessment for effectiveness and accuracy. Assessment of risk requires a thorough understanding of existing processes and of the challenges and failures. Decision making carries risk associated with several components:

1. Insufficient or faulty information regarding the decision, results, consequences, or repercussions
2. Reliance on past experiences
3. Reaching beyond the reward potential
4. Predicting the unknown
5. Predisposition to a particular outcome

The first two elements (Figure 6.3) constitute the use of faulty inputs in the decision-making process. Faulty or insufficient information leads to mishaps and diversions. Reliance on the past is useful, if placed in the context of the situation. Thinking that previous successful strategies will work flawlessly in the future is dangerous. Reaching beyond the stated objective (reward potential) is risky, given the inability to control what occurs. This risk is akin to promising more than you can deliver. Predicting the unknown is something we all strive for, but it is risky given the dynamics of everyday life. Assuming a prediction rate of 20% to 30% guarantees one in five successes, so the best advice is to predict the future with a set of contingency plans. Finally, accepting only one outcome

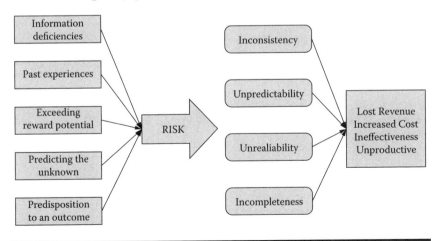

Figure 6.3 Influences and consequences of risk resulting in a negative outcome.

places a tremendous burden on others to perform. Always expecting the "best" causes structural and human issues. Leaders who expect the best place tremendous restraints on employees and resources.

Assessment of risk can take on probabilistic characteristics. This complex approach can yield valuable information. From a more practical standpoint, evaluation of risk requires an understanding of the assumptions made prior to decision making, an estimate of the risk, and the chance that negative (or neutral) outcomes occur. Figure 6.3 describes some common assumptions or presumptions before beginning the decision-making process, the presence of risk, the consequences, and overall outcomes. This method does not discount the value that knowledge and experiences bring to the decision. It is more when the decision maker relies on these alone, resulting in heightened risk.

A positive approach mitigates the risk and decreases the chance of a negative outcome. Decisions require an achievable end goal, a viable method, reliance on experience, and good judgment. Risk is always present; mitigating the risk drastically reduces unwanted outcomes. Most organizations have never truly assessed risk. Figure 6.4 details a six-step process for mitigating risk. The final step, Monitor and Control, requires a strategy for tracking the causes of risk with the objective of minimizing its effects. Finally, awareness of risk and its effect are crucial to a decision process with the goal of innovative change.

Innovation works best when decision makers consider it a process rather than an impromptu response. Decision making is more than a process: it is human endeavor that uses the mind and the intellect. When decision makers intend to achieve a positive (and innovative) outcome, they use "due process." Otherwise, the outcome is purely chance. An added dimension is the interconnectivity of the elements of decision making. Decisions affect more than the receiver, the decision maker, or the goal. Decisions affect policies and

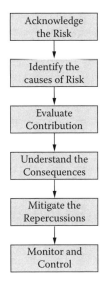

Figure 6.4   Six-step process for risk mitigation.

procedures on a microscale, often affecting the operations of other departments and services, and society on a macroscale. This effect is the reason for a more structured approach, certainly, when innovation is a concern.

Decisions that involve complex issues, such as innovation, require specific and empirical information. Rational decision making combines both experience and empirical evidence. Figure 6.5 details the steps needed to rationalize a decision.

The use of rational decision making ensures that the forecasted outcome generally succeeds. Obviously, as discussed previously, risk can modify the outcome. Rational decision making enables positive (innovative) change involving both experiential and empirical elements. Implementation of such a regimen provides employees with a sense of structure, balance, and continuity. This structure changes the paradigm of decision making. For a complete description of the positive change process, readers should consult *ENOVALE: How to Unlock Sustained Innovation Project Success* (McLaughlin and Caraballo, 2013b).

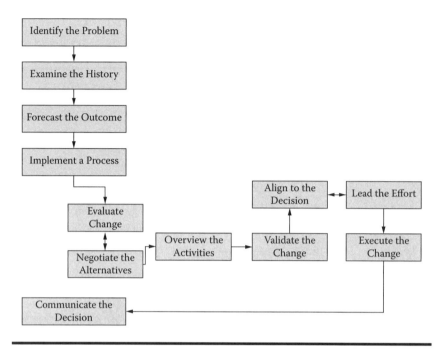

Figure 6.5   Rationalizing a decision.

Obviously, the system detailed in Figure 6.5 is not applicable for simple or recurring problems. Common sense dictates that only when the decision carries such enormous weight is there a need for such complexity. When the decision requires simplicity, then observational and experiential processes work well. This "new" paradigm of choice for decision making applies the situation concept. The problem or situation provides an opportunity to choose the complexity of decision making and ultimately affects the outcome. For "innovative change," a strategy is required. This strategy may occur only in 5% to 10% of all decisions made. When leadership or a management designee requires innovation, the strategy discussed in this book applies. For less complex decisions and outcomes, devise a hybrid of the strategy presented. With time, the healthcare leader or manager will acquire a skill that will benefit many. Even negative outcomes can be mitigated with this strategy. Consider the need to reduce the workforce (an RIF [reduction in force]). If the outcome is to minimize loss of productivity and overall employee anxiety, decisions made and executed to achieve these goals require careful thought in concert with communication, strategy, and then the actual reduction in the workforce. Although selected individuals experience a devastating loss (those who lose their jobs), the corporate psyche will suffer less and recover faster.

With risk accounted for, the final evaluation can occur. Management and the team must consider the outcome of the change. Will the outcome (1) return the process to some form of consistency (normality), (2) renew order and stability, (3) increase confidence in leadership and management, and (4) bring about a specific and measurable benefit to the organization, its customers, and stakeholders?

Finally, apply a set of criteria to the outcome as the final activity of the Validate step. The main purpose of the Validate step is to eliminate irregularities and inconsistencies, and minimize risk. Use the "IMPACT" criteria (Table 6.1) for a quick and reliable assessment. Also use this tool to overview the entire change process. Unlike the "New" and "Improve" phases, the actual change occurs during the ENOVALE™ Strategies process.

Table 6.1   IMPACT Statements

IMPACT	Less than Expected	Expected	Exceeds Expectations
Integration	Disordered	Average	Ordered
Managed change	Poor	Average	Strong
Performance	Reduced	Static	Accelerated
Acceptance	Resistance	Status quo	Acceptance
Communications	Negative	Neutral	Positive
Timeliness	Greater than 180 days	30–60 days	Less than 30 days

Step 5: Align for Best Fit

Alignment is the process of bringing together individuals to accept and support the decision and its consequences. It is not enough to support only the decision; the consequences also need support and alignment. The key to success is leadership support, acceptance of responsibility, and frequent communication. Alignment requires that both the decision (consequences) and personnel (customers/patients/users) occur in parallel for a successful implementation. Allot time for the alignment, especially if negative consequences exist. Work with resistors—those who do not want change by discussing the reasons and benefits of the decision. Some will continue to resist but these numbers will dwindle with time.

Alignment of personnel requires preparing those affected by the change. Consider the emotional and psychological aspects of change. Allow time for emotional responses. Often, serious change is much like the death of a friend that requires a period of grief, anger, acknowledgment, and acceptance. People will have issues with change—some more serious than others. Open forums are useful venues for venting feelings and emotions. Reassurance is critical with employees. Understand the emotional attachment to the existing paradigm (McLaughlin and Caraballo, 2013b). Be considerate of feelings and emotions. Permit frequent discussions regarding the decisions made, consequences, and overall results. Indicate when the change process will end. Encourage employees, customers/users, and stakeholders to submit ideas and results to mitigate negative consequences. Let people achieve equilibrium after implementing a major change. The process of acceptance varies from one decision to the next.

The alignment stage requires effective leadership and management commitment.

Innovative change will benefit many with few, if any, negative consequences. Creation of a change process accelerates progress but will also reassure stakeholders that the company can be successful in dealing with future change. Increased experience will ensure more successful implementations. Organizations that are proficient with change will succeed more often.

Step 6: Lead the Effort

Management of change is critical for outcome success. Implementation of change without a strategy can result in chaos, increased costs, and lower performance. Initializing a change management process challenges leadership and management. It is far simpler to execute a decision without a specific plan or objective, but the consequences could be devastating. In addition to leadership, management must also support and communicate the change. An organizational culture of trust, openness, and concern best facilitates change.

Change is a natural process—different and varying combinations are tried until a better "environmental" fit is found. Innovative change is not simply another "variation" but rather a leap forward leading to a better outcome. Following the ENOVALE process provides the roadmap for innovative change. Leading the effort requires a coordinated approach where the objective is clear and viable. The leader should be a skilled communicator, a dedicated visionary, a compassionate but realistic manager, and a valued and trusted employee. Often, it will not be the CEO leading the effort.

Step 7: Embrace the Change

Accept feedback and suggestions regarding the change. Let employees and customers (patients) adapt to the new environment. Time is critical—too fast and the reaction could be negative, too slow and the stakeholders lose interest. For example, the Obamacare (national healthcare coverage in the United States) debacle is a change introduced without an effective strategy, without examining or knowing the consequences, and without stakeholder support. When asked what was in the 1,000+ pages of the bill, Nancy Pelosi, Minority Leader of the US House of

Representatives, answered, "We have to pass this bill to find out what's in it." Use of the ENOVALE process could have prevented the delays, cost overruns, and general dissatisfaction that ensued.

Whether or not someone supports the healthcare initiative, the rollout process was problematic. Examining the seven-step ENOVALE Change process for the Obamacare rollout gives information on what was missed and how ENOVALE could have provided a successful rollout.

> Step 1: Evaluate the change: What reasons for this change and consequences of this change were not adequately addressed? Was a specific need defined? What about an objective?
>
> Step 2: Name the alternative: None were given; it was all or none. Those who crafted the bill did so without the input of all national healthcare stakeholders.
>
> Step 3: Overview the actions to date: Were repercussions considered? What effect would this have on stakeholders? Were all the elements and requirements clearly defined?
>
> Step 4: Validate the change: No validation was addressed, no impact was assessed, and there was no risk/reward evaluation.
>
> Step 5: Align to the decision: Congress approved the bill and everyone needed to adjust. Given the number of exclusions, alignment was never considered. Communications were poor, thus enabling a misalignment of people to the objective (the change).
>
> Step 6: Lead the effort: Leaders were difficult to identify; no time given for acceptance; reasons seemed more political than serving specific needs.
>
> Step 7: Embrace the change: Once the bill was passed, discussion ceased; it was all or nothing.

Using ENOVALE properly would have benefited all, and provided more stakeholder support and buy-in.

Change is as much the decision as it is the outcome. Change often brings about fear and anxiety. These emotions are due to our personal experiences with change that have resulted in less-than-desirable outcomes. Individuals fear change when the outcome is negative or unpredictable. This fear not only affects their emotional state, but also their behaviors. Organizations that propagate this fear do not motivate, encourage, or empower. By removing the unpredictability, the result is a process readily understood by stakeholders, permitting even acceptance of neutral or negative outcomes.

The healthcare professionals need to reevaluate their change implementation strategies. Any department or function can implement this process and achieve innovation success. The need to change will accelerate over time. How a sector or organization implements this change and achieves its outcome will greatly describe its future success. Those nimble enough to understand the dynamics of change will profit greatly. Fear and anxiety will subside, and the organization will become adaptive to the situations presented. Those left on the sidelines will waste valuable resources combating the effects of negative and neutral outcomes.

Summary

Dealing with change is both an opportunity and a threat. Change is innovative when a positive outcome exists. To achieve this outcome, a distinctive strategy is needed. This chapter detailed a strategy for innovative change customized for the healthcare sector. Not every change must be innovative, but every change should use a strategy beyond relying solely on experiences and past judgments. A strategy involves an evaluation of alternatives and consequences, an assessment of risk, validation of results, and adaptation and alignment time. The strategy requires time and effort for success. However, it greatly reduces failure, and its consequences and repercussions. The leader or manager must ask himself or herself which path is better to follow and which path, ultimately, is cost effective. With change, it all begins with the decision-making process and the amount of information known or perceived. Change is not just the decision; it is the actions that follow. Innovative change is not only possible but can occur on a frequent basis. The outcomes may not always be spectacular but the acceptance of change and its consequences will be the new organizational paradigm.

Discussion Questions

1. The old saying that nothing is constant except change depicts the healthcare industry. Change happens every day in the form of new drugs, treatments, care delivery models, decreasing reimbursement, regulations, and accrediting requirements. Analyze the use of the ENOVALE model to ensure that decisions precipitating the need for change actually contribute to a positive outcome.
2. Resistance to change is a normal response; however, leaders can mitigate resistance using a structured process. Outline ways to mitigate resistance.
3. Identify elements of risk involved in decision making. Is there a method or procedure for reducing (minimizing) risk?
4. Discuss the pros and cons of replacing a process, product, or service rather than trying to improve it. (Hint: Consider a process that changed, but not for the better.)

Assignment

1. Consider a recent decision (could be personal or business related). Identify two or more alternatives. What were the repercussions of each alternative?
2. Pick a change that occurred recently. Did it significantly improve output? If not, try to diagnose the reasons for the less-than-expected performance.
3. Describe in a paragraph why management should remain actively involved in decision making.
4. Describe a change in your life that could be considered innovative (by yourself and those who know you).

Chapter 7

Defining and Measuring Success

Introduction

Numerous studies and factual evidence, as measured by corporations, have directly tied *innovation* to increased performance. However, investment in the innovation is critical as well. Poor funding or inadequate resources influence innovation's eventual success (Paladino, 2009). Inevitably, the innovation must perform and provide a benefit. Measuring this performance, benefit, and value becomes the reason for this chapter.

Organizations recognize that for innovation to be successful, there must be a financial benefit achieved. Whether that benefit is competitive advantage, significant cost savings, increased revenues, or ROI (return on investment), innovation must produce a tangible advantage to the organization as well as to the user, shareholder, and stakeholder. Innovation must maximize the payback of the investment made (Jana, 2007). The value of the innovation also has a tremendous effect on financial performance. Limited value returns less payback and fewer competitive advantages but could easily satisfy social, environmental, or governance requirements (Eccles and Serafeim, 2013). Therefore, the concept and measurement of innovation's value and success need definition prior to beginning the innovation project. This agrees well with the philosophy of Global Targeting, Inc.

The for-profit organizations understand the reality of investing hundreds of billions of dollars in innovations. Oftentimes, the success rate is a mere 10% or less. Even technologically innovated companies, such as P&G, may have only 15% of projects meeting cost and revenue targets (Brown and Anthony, 2011). Yet, these successes drive future projects and future advances. Innovations, however, have both tangible and intangible measures of success, many of which are not financially related. Value also represents a measure of success/performance that can exceed expectations. Many nonprofit organizations consider value the most powerful outcome to provide a customer/user or patient.

Measures of value and success vary from one industry sector to another. Technological advances, new applications, and new approaches use measures of financial performance to judge success. Yet other less-tangible measures are also critical for assessing innovation success. These measures may be just as critical as revenues and ROI, but are not financially driven. Measures such as motivation, retention, and productivity are just as critical for measuring success. This is especially true in the not-for-profit healthcare sector businesses and organizations. In the healthcare industry, recognition of value and success happens in many different ways. Every year, Truven Health Analytics reviews the performance of the 5,000 hospitals in the United States and awards honors to those that have achieved both the highest current performance and the fastest long-term improvement over 5 years. *US News & World Report* annually surveys 5,000 US hospitals using 10,000 specialists to review the data on death rates, patient safety, and hospital reputation for a total of 147 parameters. The Leapfrog

Group, comprised of employers, compares hospitals regarding patient outcomes, the use of resources, and how leadership promotes patient safety. In addition, the government publishes Hospital Compare Data on 4,000 Medicare-certified hospitals. The Dartmouth studies focus on Medicare data that is used to compare the use of resources used in local, regional, and national areas. The study compares the usage of resources with the outcomes, which are published for use by government agencies, payers, and other researchers. The diversity of the elements studied by the researchers in these various organizations signifies success in specific areas without any focus on the financial viability of the organization.

Every sector has its own specific and unique measures of success. Research and practice have shown that innovation has a positive impact on the growth, success, and survival of the organization (Bigliardi, 2013). As stated previously, success for some is financial; for others, it is goal oriented; and for others, it is value or accomplishment. How an organization defines and measures success is critical to innovation. Each project may require a small number of unique measurements related to its success criteria. This chapter discusses how to define success and creates a set of measurements, all based on a set of performance goals.

Defining Success

Success is attained when a goal or objective is achieved. The objective must link to the end user (customer or patient), who ultimately decides whether the item is innovative. Success, therefore, must define satisfaction with the item. Innovative success adds the dimension of need: it must fulfill a need by convincing the customers (patients) to change their purchase behaviors or satisfaction with the item.

As part of the ENOVALE™ Solutions phase, a definition of success preceded the establishment of the objective. Expressing innovation success takes on the form of

- Customer/patient/user terms (what individual needs are satisfied)
- Functional terms (how it will perform versus existing standards)
- Business or organizational terms (how the business thrives and grows)

Given the breadth of the sector, each subsector (e.g., home healthcare, diagnostics) would have its own distinctive success criteria. This could easily mean that different subsectors could use measures of success (failure) that could be defined uniquely for that subsector need. The term "mortality rates" could have very distinct meanings in each of healthcare's numerous subsectors. This is one reason why financial measures are so easily adaptable across the sector. Once the team knows what it wants to accomplish, it can finalize a definition of success. Success in patient-oriented healthcare would include what the patient needs, wants, and desires, and how the visit, treatment, or procedure performs compared to expectations and experiences.

After defining success, the project objective can be formalized. Key success measures are incorporated into the objective. The initial team of managerial, technical, and financial personnel must review and approve these criteria to proceed. Framing the definition of success leaves little room for drastic changes that can cause major delays. This simple exercise provides a rallying point for the team and helps to align others to the intent of the innovation.

Defining success must translate into a traceable measure. The measure must provide a valid and reliable assessment of the success criteria. Use the KISS principle when determining what and how to measure: K-Keep, I-It, S-Simple, and S-Straightforward.

Creating Measurements

A typical for-profit healthcare sector business often measures sales, costs, brand awareness, ROI (return on investment), etc., yet measures such as employee motivation and resilience of the business may provide useful indicators as well (Eccles and Serafeim, 2013). Others see innovation's success as the amount of payback on the investment made (Jana, 2007). However, for innovation to be successful, it must return a significant financial benefit while providing distinctive differentiation between itself and its competitors (Hull and Rothenberg, 2008). Shulman (2006) recommends that ROI be defined prior to introducing the innovation. There is no lack of measurement when it comes to assessing project value from financial perspective.

Financial measures are the most common and well developed. These crucial measures determine the viability of the innovation. Most financial measures are lagging and internally based. Innovation requires a strong external focus, given its dependence on needs, experiences, and knowledge of the customer (patient) or user. Therefore, a blend of measures should truly reflect the potential of the innovation.

Additional measures of success in the healthcare sector can consist of

- Cost savings, profit, competitive advantage, and ROI (financial and business focused)
- Length of stay, recovery time, satisfaction, value, purchasing behaviors (patient/customer focused)
- Efficiency, effectiveness, quality, process and production (functionally focused)
- Productivity, motivation, attitude (human or employee focused)

Understanding the concept of innovation requires knowledge, experience, and a specific measure of performance (success). Performance is a metric, such as patient satisfaction; success is a judgment of accomplishment. Therefore, patient satisfaction can increase (decrease) and be judged successful, or not. Innovation is judged successful when expectations are exceeded and unfulfilled (unsatisfied) needs are met. Success requires a definition that incorporates a measure of performance that exceeds expectations and meets an outstanding need. For example, it is not enough to know that a profit exists, but that the profit meets the criteria of success. For-profits need to make a profit to exist and grow. Capturing significant market share, while making a profit, may define innovation success. This is a critical need for pharmaceutical or medical products companies. To summarize, individuals must acknowledge the success (experience the increase in performance), have their expectations exceeded, and fulfill a need to be innovative.

Project Success

Once success is defined and measured, the team can begin ranking the importance of each measure. Identification of key performance metrics (often referred to as KPVs—key performance variables) is critical in the initial phases. KPVs require tracking, analysis, and evaluation. KPVs may change as the project progresses, as the importance of certain elements changes. Another indicator of performance is a KPI (key performance indicator). These KPI metrics are closely related to goal or target values. These generally do not change and are regarded as standards. Characteristics of KPIs (Todorvic, Mitrovic, and Bjelica [2013]) include

1. Fully accountable, easy to understand, practical
2. Timely, accurate

Figure 7.1   KPI creation process. (Adapted from Todorvic, M., Mitrovic, Z., and Bjelica, D. *Journal for Theory and Practice Management,* 68, 41–48, 2013.)

3. Actionable
4. Relevant; directly related to financial performance
5. Predictive

Creating KPIs is a step-wise process; see Figure 7.1.

KPIs are used to judge performance and may be used individually or combined to assess project success. More in-depth measures provide project assessment. Todorvice, Mitrovic, and Bjelica (2013) detail integrated performance indicators (IPIs) as a method of assessing various phases of a project. Without providing the details, these IPIs are combinations of KPIs. Consult their article for more details.

Project success (Table 7.1) is based on many attributes, not just the measurement of KPIs. Using the Project Management Institute's Body of Knowledge (PMBOK®) document, Turner and Zolin (2012) list a series of measures (metrics) necessary for project success. These are certainly applicable for innovation projects and demonstrate the breadth of measures needed to properly assess a project's overall worthiness.

Traditional project success measures may not be fully integrated with innovation project needs. One technique, called Earned Value Management, focuses on planned accomplishments (expenditures) and actual cost. Earned Value goes one step further and examines the actual accomplishment (Sharma, 2013). The PMBOK defines Earned Value Management (EVM) as a method that integrates scope, schedule, and resources for measuring project performance. EVM compares the amount of work that was planned with what has been spent and with what has been accomplished to determine cost and schedule performance (Sharma, 2013).

Table 7.1 Five Categories of Project Success

Efficiency	Impact on Team	Impact on Customer	Business Success	Preparation for the Future
Meeting schedule	Team satisfaction	Meeting requirements	Sales	New technology
Meeting cost	Team morale	Meeting specification	Profits	New market
Yield, performance, functionality	Skill	Benefit to the customer	Market share	New product line
	Team member growth	Extent of use	ROI, ROE	New core competency
Other denied efficiencies	Team member retention	Customer satisfaction	Cash flow	New organizational capability
	No burnout	Customer loyalty	Service quality	
		Brand-name recognition	Cycle time	
			Organizational measures	
			Regulatory approval	

Source: Adapted from Shenhar, A. J., and Dvir, D. (2007). *Reinventing Project Management: The Diamond Approach to Successful Growth and Innovation.* Boston, MA: Harvard Business School Press.

EVM gives management further insights into risks (a key determinant of innovation), permitting a risk mitigation plan. EVM can be thought of as an "early warning "program (Sharma, 2013); it uses traditional accounting measures such as schedule variance, cost variance, performance indices, cost performance, critical ratios, etc. EVM analysis is used as a tool for cost control; it is helpful in determining how the project progresses, in terms of cost, scope, and time, determining whether the cost is under control or it will go over the planned budget or the time required if the project continues working at the same pace (Sharma, 2013). Finally, EVM provides an evaluation of the final cost, permits change control, and keeps management informed of the overall project viability.

In addition, Global Targeting, Inc. has developed software and applications to enter, track, and evaluate these measures, both on project and enterprise versions. Information is available on the organization's website at www.globaltargeting.com.

After defining and selecting the measures of success, the project can move forward. These measures provide a means of evaluation and are developed during the ENOVALE Solutions phase. The link to performance is a critical step, given that innovation without success is unsustainable. At the project stage, measures are often enhanced and modified. However, the objective remains the same. For nonprofits, substitute the word "value" for "success." An innovation must bring lasting value, tied to performance or accomplishment.

The remainder of this chapter discusses success (performance) measures for various healthcare subsectors. All organizations share a great deal of commonality in measuring performance; it is these measures from which we define innovation performance and success. For example, the Centers for Medicare & Medicaid Services (CMS) decided that patients should also rate their healthcare. In order to capture the patient perspective, the government created the Hospital Consumer Assessment of Healthcare Providers and Systems (HCAHPS). The results of these scores determine the payment amounts the government issues to hospitals based on patient satisfaction as assessed in the HCAHPS scores. Hospitals are penalized 2% if they do not meet the required satisfaction score. In 2013, some 1,450 hospitals received the 2% penalty (Rau, 2013).

Each of the entities that rates hospitals used different parameters to measure their success. While some may think that success comes from name recognition and patients may make choices about their care based on name recognition, the various studies show that these organizations may not provide the highest quality of care, nor may they deliver it in the most cost effective manner. Studies like these argue for a more effective method of project tracking.

Some kind of innovation is necessary to improve the scores collected by various entities. Less-than-stellar performance that generates sustained success is innovative, if judged by individuals. This sustained success is where it becomes difficult for the producer to know if an item will be judged as innovative. Feedback from customer/patients is combined with needs analysis derived from both structured and unstructured data using analytics.

Cost and Benefits

Studies from Dartmouth (2010) compare care delivery, identify regional and local differences in costs, and then correlate the data with the outcomes. For example, the study identifies differences in the types of care and the cost. In a state-by-state comparison, Dartmouth compares the number of total mastectomies versus partial mastectomies. Then it looks at survival rates and determines if the more radical surgery, which costs more and takes longer for healing to occur, produces better outcomes in terms of reoccurrence of cancer and longevity. See Figure 7.2.

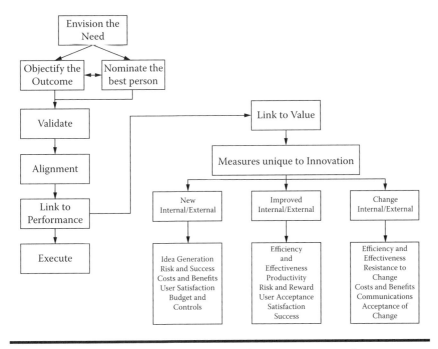

Figure 7.2   Links to generic measures of performance and success.

Critical Healthcare Measures

Traditionally, hospitals focused on acquiring the latest technology and physicians who could use this technology, as evidenced by the spread of the daVinci® robot for surgery. Hospitals based their advertising on this acquisition and touted the rationale for using it. However, a study showed that while the growth of use was about 10% since 2007, the outcomes were questionable that the technique provided more quality while significantly increasing the cost of the procedures. A daVinci robot costs $125,000 initially and requires expensive annual maintenance contracts. It does, however, fit the new internal/external innovation requirement.

Effectiveness

In healthcare, *effectiveness* is measured by the outcome, meaning an improved health status due to prevention or intervention. For example, scientific studies compare the use of cardiac stents with open-heart surgery. Four years post-procedure, open-heart surgery patients had less stroke incidence and a lower risk of subsequent heart attacks than those who received a cardiac stent (Brasseur, 2013). This was the reason for the development of drug-eluting stents.

Value (Patient Satisfaction)

Each group that evaluates hospitals on cost, quality, and outcome publishes this information in order to focus on some aspect of perceived value. As described previously in this chapter, the HCAHPS provides patient satisfaction data from the patient's perspective, The Leapfrog group looks at cost and outcome from the employer cost perspective, both measuring overall value. The government publishes the Hospital Compare Data to provide information to patients as they make a "valued" decision about physicians and facilities for their choice of care.

Reputation

Truven Health Analytics (Ann Arbor, Michigan) and *US News* reports provide data and information that these physicians and facilities can use as part of their reputation. A positive reputation will attract employees, reduce employee turnover, improve customer attitudes, lower risk, and create higher credibility (Davies, Chun, and Kamins, 2010). A positive reputation provides a distinct competitive advantage (Davies, Chun, and Kamins, 2010). Hospitals often hang posters in their lobbies and use electronic billboards to publish where they rank in these studies. For those interested in brand loyalty and brand awareness, reputation is a key for success. Reputation is difficult to quantify but is important for those in the healthcare sector. It is often a make-or-break situation when reputation is the only key variable used to make a decision.

For the healthcare sector dedicated to manufacturing, pharmaceuticals, and diagnostics, innovation success is achieved by exceeding a prescribed set of financial, customer, and competitive goals. For these industries, competitive advantage is as critical as reputation as it measures overall effectiveness in holding market share. Each business and each organization will have its own unique measures of performance and success.

Summary

All projects need distinctive measures of success. These will vary by sector, business, product, and service offering. This chapter described why success and performance metrics need to encompass more than just financial performance. Both internal and external measures describe the product, service, or technology from its conception to completion. Measures must include those potentially used by the consumers to judge innovation, measures to evaluate function and use, and measures unique to the business or organization.

The number, diversity, and reason for measures in the healthcare sector are huge. This chapter provided a brief overview of performance measures and the need for both accuracy and consistency. Measures were identified and developed for specific reasons with an emphasis on healthcare-related industry indicators. This book's purpose is not to explain how to create detailed measures and evaluate these for efficacy, but rather to stress the need for effective measures when involved in the innovation process. Without these measures, assessment and validation are impossible. Using available measures, without understanding innovation unique strategy, provides only a glimpse of the total picture. So often, measures are the last item considered; and yet without these measures, success is never truly or precisely defined—inevitably, a true loss for innovation.

Discussion Questions

1. Define "success" as it applies to your organization or business. Is success measured effectively?
2. How do performance and success relate to one another? Consider an example as a way to explain this relationship.
3. Identify and define three KPVs (KPIs) in your organization or business. Are these leading or lagging indicators? If lagging, what can be done to make these more of a "leading" measure?
4. Discuss the concept of value in your organization. Is value clearly communicated throughout your organization?

Assignment

1. How would you express innovation success regarding
   a. Customer/patient/user terms (what individual needs are satisfied)?
   b. Functional terms (how will it perform versus existing standards)?
   c. Business or organizational terms (how the business thrives and grows)?
2. For innovation success, described in Question 1, define at least two measures for each of the three elements.
3. Select success criteria, and use the KISS principle to develop measures of success.

Chapter 8

Future of Innovation in Healthcare

Introduction

The future is always difficult to predict, given the dynamics of a changing society. Futurists study patterns and trends, and then try to extrapolate the future of these patterns and trends; but trends, by nature, never continue. There will always be a reversal, and sometimes it will be abrupt. Does that mean that interest in innovation will wane in the future, or will it take a different direction, producing a different outcome?

Innovation will be a critical organizational strategy in 20 to 30 years. We predict it will be more integrated than at present, and people will have the opportunity to participate in the process, at will. Innovation training and certification will be common. Whole countries will embrace the concept of innovation; business will implement innovation to expand their marketshare; people will freely participate on project teams to meet unsatisfied needs. Innovation training, experience, and certification will become a distinguishing factor and an outward sign of high commitment to quality. The future trend is to move away from the innovation as a "grand scheme" to an evolutionary approach that requires holistic thinking, and attention to all who participate in the innovation ecosystem (Hamer, Plochg, and Moreira, 2012).

It seems that most see the future as worse than today, some better than today, but few see little change. In fact, most of human history is speckled with big events that change society; otherwise change is slow but deliberate. Discoveries, inventions, and innovation will continue to permeate the healthcare sector. This chapter explores some of these innovations and puts them into a perspective of how the future will unfold.

To Know the Future, Assess the Present and Learn from the Past

It is often said that societies easily repeat the failures of the past. This saying comes from arrogance and a lack of understanding of history. Corporations, not-for-profits, and facilities/groups often make the same mistake. These organizations will say that large amounts of investment dollars were spent on improvement projects but with little or nothing to show for it 2 years later. In fact, for healthcare, less than 50% of quality improvement projects were ever implemented (Hamer, Plochg, and Moreira, 2012). Therefore, spending valuable resources on innovation seems unwarranted. Here, the past is influencing the present—but the reasoning and logic does not quite apply to innovation, for which the goals and objectives differ greatly from past projects.

To plan resource allocations, most firms assume that the future is similar to the present; but what if the competition plans to assume a larger market share due to the introduction of innovative products? Then, the assumption is faulty, and the money potentially wasted with a less-than-satisfactory ROI (return on investment). Consider that an organization that scans the environment and understands what innovation can do has plans for introducing its own innovation, thus disrupting the marketplace. This organization "molds" the future by seeding its success with innovation in the present. The learning is that what exists today will work tomorrow. Consider the examples that follow.

Healthcare leaders face declining reimbursement along with global payments under the Patient Protection and Affordable Care Act (PPACA), an aging population that requires more care, a shortage of primary care physicians, and a projected shortage of allied health personnel (nurses, pharmacists, physical therapists, etc.). In other words, more care required with less money to deliver the care and with less resources.

The Institute of Medicine (2010) noted in their study on the future of nursing that the places where nurses practice continue to move away from the acute care setting in hospitals to ambulatory care settings, home care, clinics, community, long-term care, and schools. In addition, the field of advanced practice nursing and physician assistants continues to increase. In 1995, 23% of nurses practiced at the acute care level; and in 2009, 48% practiced in this expanded role. The report emphasized an education pathway for nurses' aides and practical nurses to follow to meet the highest level of practice. The study also emphasized the need for more bachelors-degree prepared nurses. The researchers noted that nurses could take over much of the primary care provided to patients with a focus on prevention and chronic disease management. They also need to assume a role in boardrooms and in other leadership positions.

In order for nursing to move into these new roles, innovation needs to occur. The accountabilities of advanced practice and close relationships with physicians and other allied health personnel require the focused, structured innovation techniques of ENOVALE™.

Under global payments in the PPACA, hospitals, physicians, and allied healthcare providers receive one payment for maintaining the health of the population they serve. At the present time, hospitals, physicians, pharmacies, and other providers bill separately for all the services they provide for a patient in terms of treatment, prevention, or intervention. However, the PPACA focuses on population health (wellness). Eventually, they will receive one payment for keeping an individual healthy, independent of any treatments the patient requires.

The Centers for Medicare & Medicaid Services (CMS) continues to add to the list of never-events that receive no reimbursement when they occur. The idea behind no reimbursement is that the event should never happen, and if it did, an unsafe practice occurred. Coordination of post-discharge care ensures that patients are not readmitted. Once treated, patients should be discharged in a condition for healing. The CMS emphasizes the need to prevent readmission of patients on the original list that included heart failure, pneumonia, and heart attack. They also added new categories that include total hip and knee replacement patients, along with chronic obstructive pulmonary disease. The rationale for adding these new conditions was volume, as 1.4 million total joint replacement procedures are performed annually. They are also the largest procedural cost in the Medicare payment budget (Clark, 2014).

Understanding the Present Situation

Hospital pricing for the same procedure, treatment, and hospital stay varies widely across the United States. The Dartmouth World Atlas (2010) studies show no difference in patient outcome attributed to the cost disparities. For this reason, the CMS will focus more acutely on hospital charges and costs. Due to increased scrutiny, many hospitals have reviewed procedures and orders that provide no proven value or benefit to patient outcomes. Part of this scrutiny includes the use of blood products for transfusions. The cost and value of tests and treatments means that physicians need more education on the cost of tests and treatments in order to determine if the cost/benefit adds value to diagnosis or treatment.

Due to declining reimbursements, many hospital strategic plans include tactics to reduce costs by 20% to 30% every year for 3 to 5 years. The cuts to reimbursement to hospitals were defined in the PPACA. Hospitals and providers know it is coming because the way to fund the provisions of the PPACA is through these reductions. The goal of the PPACA is to expand healthcare coverage (access), improve the delivery system and outcomes (value-based care), and at the same time control costs. With global payments, management will need to foster innovation to use resources wisely, improve the revenue cycle, improve supply-chain management, and redefine the roles of individuals as the organization delivers healthcare.

Employers, physicians, and consumers all think the cost of healthcare is too high, and 65% of respondents in these three categories grade the quality of care provided at a "C" (Deloitte, 2012). Interestingly enough, employers and consumers blame the high cost of care on hospitals, while hospitals blame the costs on patient behaviors (Deloitte, 2012).

The timeline in the PPACA includes an expansion of Medicaid (low payments for service) and another decrease in Medicare payments. Due to the high deductibles in commercial insurance plans provided by employers and the government healthcare exchanges, hospitals will incur more bad debt along with an increase in charity care (Heckley, 2014).

At the same time the government is changing the reimbursement model from fee-for-service to value-based purchasing, hospitals are facing more competition from physicians who add technology to their offices and clinics, and take away ancillary testing and minimally invasive procedures. They frequently target the well-insured and send patients with Medicaid, Medicare, and charity needs to nonprofit hospitals that are required to provide care in order to keep their nonprofit status. This strategy on the part of physicians also decreases the margin and financial viability of the hospitals. These hospitals will only survive by using innovation.

All these changes will require providers to develop new, innovative ways of maintaining and improving the health of each individual in a service area (population health). The change from a focus on illness to wellness and the changing role of providers and allied health personnel require innovation.

Future of Healthcare Innovation

"The future of healthcare needs to shift to what people need, not what the current system needs. And it should shift to one of paying doctors for the health and well-being of people and patients, instead of the current emphasis on illness care and fee for service that is more costly" (Wood, 2014). The present system of policies and reimbursement models drives current thinking and prevents healthcare professionals from meeting the needs of patients (Wood, 2014).

Implications for Future Innovation

Changes to Delivery

The PPACA of 2010 included a provision for Accountable Care Organizations (ACOs). These organizations include hospitals, clinics, ambulatory care centers, and independent physician offices that integrate into one health system with responsibility for the total care of the patient. The ACO focuses on the continuum of care rather than the episodic care of the past where the patient was treated for the chief complaint provided at the time of the encounter. The "chief complaint" way of providing care meant that physicians often prescribed medications that did not work together and often caused other problems.

Tests were duplicated and often the patient was notified of problems noted in results of tests.

Instead of providing episodic care in silos, care will happen using teams of people working together and across entities to provide patient-focused care. The PPACA also includes the need for medical homes where a primary care physician over-sees and coordinates all care received by the patient.

Payers (insurance) previously contracted for the best rates for patient care services. Now, the focus shifts to collaborating with the providers and including the patient in all treatment decisions. Patients will need to take more responsibility for their own health status.

Payment Reform

The PPACA includes a provision for bundled payments, mean-ing that instead of paying physicians, a lab, and the facility for providing care for an episode, the bundled payment will be shared by all these providers. In addition, hospitals receive no payment for readmissions within 30 days of discharge. This penalty creates another reason for hospitals to expand their scope to include homecare and long-term care. The acquisition of these entities helps the hospital work more closely on the post-discharge care to avoid these readmissions. It also cre-ates the need to connect these entities to the electronic record software used by the hospital to ensure that post-discharge caregivers have all the information they need.

The payment shifts from recognizing the activity provided to and for the patient to outcomes, which means more focus on value rather than volume. The PPACA calls this shift "value-based purchasing." These outcomes include both achievement of optimal function and fewer complications resulting from care. Of course, providers also received the task of lowering costs and increasing quality at the same time.

The newest proposed legislation for Medicare, The Better Care, Lower Cost Act of 2014 (Wyden, 2014), proposed funding of teams that can focus on strategies for improving the patient's health while lowering the overall cost of their care. The idea behind this legislation is to avoid cutting payments to either beneficiaries or providers. Instead, it creates an incentive for more coordinated and efficient care.

In addition to decreasing the Medicaid payment, the US Congress also plans to eliminate the Disproportionate Share Hospital payment for those that care for more Medicaid patients than the average hospital.

Population Health

The US healthcare system was built on identification of disease, treating disease, and, in some cases, preventing disease. Interventions occurred to correct the outcome of disease or trauma. With population health, the focus shifts from a system focused on sickness and disability to one focused on wellness and optimal function. To accomplish this goal, the lines will blur between health and social issues. Wellness requires coordination of social services and health services. People who cannot take off work to make a preventive appointment or for chronic disease maintenance do not achieve optimal health and function.

Mount Sinai Hospital, in New York City, serves a large Medicaid population. Their studies (Johnson, 2014) show that senior patients' ability to maintain their own health status is affected for those living in housing with broken elevators and other problems. They decided to tackle these problems as part of population health. Their studies show that unemployment, homelessness, and poverty affect a person's health, and they are collaborating with others to solve this problem (Johnson, 2014).

Electronic Medical Records

The electronic medical record (EMR) ensures that the patient's complete history is readily available to any and every provider in order to eliminate duplicate tests and ensure safety. At the same time, patients want privacy along with coordinated care. The challenge is how to ensure that the record is available but not viewed improperly.

The PPACA also includes a dimension called *interoperability,* meaning that every piece of medical software includes design features that make it possible to integrate information from every other piece of software in order to create a longitudinal picture of the patient's care and health status. Most organizations that have adopted an EMR found that only 20% of the adoption was technical, while the other 80% involved adaptive change and integrating the previous operational systems with the new technology (Mace, 2014).

One of the biggest advantages of the electronic EMR is the ability to incorporate clinical decision support into physician orders. In other words, decision support checks orders for patients to ensure they are appropriate and complete based on the information entered into the record. The program checks for allergies and drug-drug interactions, and creates alerts if any of the information and orders do not align.

When providers were surveyed as to their information technology (IT) priorities, 39% of hospitals plan to target care coordination, while 51% of health systems included this target in their plans. These two groups also reported that 32% plan to invest in clinical decision support (Zeis, 2013).

Analytics

Now that all the patient care information resides in a repository, it is possible to analyze care and decide on the lowest-cost treatment that produces the best outcome. The data also highlights the highest-cost patients who need more care and the physicians who use the most-expensive treatments.

Intermountain Healthcare in Salt Lake City, Utah, initiated its electronic medical record 40 years ago and now has a repository containing 2 trillion unique medical data elements along with interactions with vendors, manufacturers, payers, hospitals, and physicians. They plan to analyze this information in order to further refine their healthcare system.

Deloitte (Monegain, 2014) recently started a new business unit focused on data from Intermountain with the following goals:

1. Clinical and operational excellence: analytics, services, and insights to enable health systems to help optimize business and clinical processes, reduce variation, enhance programs, and improve patient safety, productivity and margin to offer higher quality care with lower costs.
2. Value-based care: solutions and insights to improve population health management and clinical outcomes, manage risk, reduce unwarranted variation, coordinate care, leverage evidence-based guidelines, and support new reimbursement models.
3. Research excellence: solutions and insights to improve clinical and translational research capabilities; enable personalized, genomic medicine; support comparative effectiveness analyses leveraging real-world evidence; and improve safety and disease surveillance programs.

Along those same lines, McKinsey & Company started their own business unit using data from Adventist HealthCare system's repository of data. Their premise is that achieving goals regarding population health and accountable care can only occur using robust analytics technology. The goals of accountable care, and population health cannot fully be achieved without advanced data collection and reporting systems. To make these goals, ACOs will use data to correlate clinical data and claims data. The analysis will identify the actions and plans necessary to manage population health. Many organizations possess this data; however, few possess the skills and knowledge to use it effectively (Mace, 2013).

Artificial intelligence combined with natural language processing makes it possible to provide analytics that can improve the diagnosis of images. The computer learns to identify patterns, identifies them, and alerts radiologists to ensure detection of more abnormalities than they would without the use of a computer. Clinical decision support has advanced in other areas of medicine and now moves forward into the world of the radiologist (Kim, 2013).

Personnel Changes and Expanded Roles

Over the past several years, healthcare added tens of thousands of jobs every month. At the end of 2013, hiring slowed and is expected to continue to decline. Hospital leaders in particular expect to decrease the number of employees. Nursing homes eliminated 1,000 jobs a month in 2013 and expect this trend to continue. Instead, the insurance agency will continue to add jobs based on the changes precipitated by the PPACA (Evans, 2014). Instead of providing episodic care in silos, care will happen with teams using the expertise of each team member and allowing each team member to function to the extent of his or her professional license.

More physicians accept employment from hospitals. In 2006, 16% of physicians were employed by hospitals. Just 6 years later, 26% accepted an employment agreement with a hospital. These previously autonomous physicians need to adapt to employment where they must follow the rules of the organization instead of making their own employment rules. At the same time that these physicians convert from independent practitioner to employee, they also find themselves working side-by-side with the millennial generation who need to create a new culture of cooperation. A generation ago, most physicians were male, and now the ranks consist of a 50% male/female mix. Women traditionally choose to work part-time.

As legislation and accreditation move forward to emphasize collaboration between various providers, hospitals recruit physicians for their clinical skills. They are moving into leadership roles where new clinical management structures focus on efficiently reducing waste, using scarce resources appropriately along with strong goals on clinical quality and patient centricity (Combes, 2014).

At the same time, leaders face the need to engage these newly employed physicians. Leaders feel a need to create standards for productivity, efficacy, timeliness, and patient satisfaction, while historically physicians had little oversight and only received reviews of their work if the deviation created a malpractice case or similar issue. Hospital leadership needs tools and techniques to make this transition favorable for all involved.

Eliminate Waste and Improve Processes

Hospitals increasingly engage physicians in discussions about what instruments, equipment, and supplies are needed to conduct a procedure. Vendors provide volume discounts for standardization. The more standardization, the higher the volume and, in turn, the higher the discount becomes. During the standardization discussions with physicians, another topic is that of eliminating waste. Too often in the past, the standardization included everything physicians ever wanted. Now, the focus is on truly deciding on a minimal amount of supplies in a pack and opening additional items only as needed and, thereby, eliminating waste caused by discarded, unused products.

A new target for eliminating waste involves the ordering of imaging studies. Too often, studies occurred that did not provide valuable information for diagnosis. As an example, physicians looked at the standard for ordering MRIs (magnetic resonance images) on patients with back pain (Robeznieks, 2014). But only a small percentage of these studies provided any usable information for treatment decisions. Therefore, Virginia Mason Medical Center in Seattle eliminated MRIs from their back pain order sets (Robeznieks, 2014).

Suppliers

Historically, manufacturers of medical devices developed relationships with physicians who would order their products. Hospitals were at the mercy of these orders. However, during the past decade, hospital leaders have focused more on the standardization of products to save money. The next change involves contracting that includes value-added services and supplies at a set dollar amount.

At other times, evaluation of the service may prove unnecessary. For example, total joint implants were typically brought to the operating room by a sales representative who stayed with the implant during surgery and developed a relationship with the surgeon, who would use the same implant over and over again. The surgeon really did not need the service of the sales rep. Now, implant manufacturers also offer implants without the sales rep service, which reduces the cost of the implant by 50% compared to that with sales rep accompaniment (Lee, 2013).

One area that never received much attention was an area called "other purchased services," which encapsulates acquisitions that are not related to equipment, capital, or staff. Heartland Health decided to evaluate every one of these agreements and found they could renegotiate these contracts to save $2 million in the first year. The savings came from copiers, software licenses, and consulting services (Molpus, 2013).

Increasing Safety

Patient monitoring devices contain alarms that ring to alert the nurse that a patient needs help. However, the ringing alarms often mean nothing, and patients learn how to silence them. As of January 2014, The Joint Commission added a new safety goal: to decrease alarm fatigue and to ensure that when an alarm occurred, that someone checked it. The root cause of alarm fatigue and silence was that alarms were set as warnings, and the warnings were ignored. Boston Medical Center decided to address the issue and created a policy that changed all alarm settings to identification of a true problem requiring a nurse to review the alarm. Often, this change meant setting the ranges to longer intervals. They also created a policy wherein two nurses could review an individual patient's values and set the alarm to more closely match the patient's rates. They were able to create a safer environment and at the same time eliminate alarm fatigue (McKinney, 2014).

Patient Experience

The theme for patients in legislation and accreditation involves patients taking responsibility for their own health. However, the payers also monitor patient satisfaction scores and provide incentive payments for improved scores. Another key innovation underway is called a "Patient Led Approach." The movement is to put the needs of the patient at the forefront of innovation (McNichol, 2012). The World Health Organization (WHO) has said that by 2020, people will

- Make use of their own assets
- Be active participants in shaping health policy
- Respond to the health challenges by improving health literacy
- Ensure their voice in patient-centered health systems
- Participate fully in community and family life (McNichol, 2012)

Changing Roles

Tim Porter O'Grady espouses the theory that nurses will play a critical role in the new focus on health rather than sickness. Nurses already possess well-established competencies focused on coordinating and integrating care, while developing strong relationships with patients (Porter O'Grady, 2014). Registered nurses already fill the role of case manager, one who ensures that patients receive care in a timely manner. They routinely manage a group of patients with a chronic condition to ensure their condition stays within normal limits, and they quickly intervene if physiological changes occur. A new role is one of patient navigator, one who ensures coordination of patient care between providers, patients, and populations (Dougwood, 2014). They may also coordinate care among providers to ensure optimal care and seamless hand-offs between services. While evidence-based medicine provides for standardized care, nurses customize the standardization to meet the specific needs of individual patients.

Predictions

Healthcare costs and outcomes are on the radar screen of employers, the government, and individuals. Patients, payors, and providers all recognize that scarce resource allocation must go to those who will benefit the most. The elected officials are looking at making those with more money pay more for services. They also implemented value-based purchasing, which is another method of conducting a cost/benefit analysis. In other words, what is the outcome and value for every expenditure?

As individuals pay more out-of-pocket expenses for their own care, they will increasingly want to know what they are getting for their money. Patients and payers want to know costs upfront in order to comparison shop for the best value for the money. In order to afford premiums and co-pays, patients want transparency on costs and outcomes. Several websites provide quality comparisons online now. This transparency will increase as individuals pay more attention to them. It will create more competition for lower costs and higher quality.

The aging of the US population is predicted to escalate the monies spent on this population. Unfortunately, many seniors acquired conditions such as heart disease, diabetes, and hypertension due to unhealthy lifestyles. These conditions combined with obesity cause damage to joints (causing a need for replacement) and organs (requiring repair, replacement, and/or dialysis). Instead of taking control of their own health status, they sought treatments and drugs to make them feel better. The new focus is on bringing these conditions to within normal limits through diet and exercise, and engaging them in monitoring their own physiological signs. This trend will continue.

The senior population also watched their parents suffer through chemotherapy that extended life but came with diminished quality. The baby boomers always want control; they will reject lifesaving treatments that diminish the quality of life and instead will seek palliative and hospice care to make them comfortable instead of prolonging life in agony.

At the same time, individuals are encouraged to monitor their own diet and exercises through the use of apps on their smartphones. They can log the number of steps taken daily, enter the calories, and see if they ate more than they exercised, thus resulting in weight gain. Apps also monitor blood sugar, heart rate, and other parameters. Individuals learn what foods and activities increase their well-being. Instead of medicines for irritable bowel syndrome, patients are encouraged to add yogurt to their diet to create more normal flora in the bowel.

Medicare has calculated that 32% of its patients possess two or three chronic conditions, 23% have four or five, and 14% have six or more of these chronic conditions; they account for 80% of the growth in costs to care for the total senior population. Medicare beneficiaries with two or three chronic conditions cost $5,700 per year, four or five chronic conditions cost $9,800 per year, and six or more chronic conditions cost $33,000 per year (Barr, 2014).

These numbers were collected and analyzed from the vast amount of data submitted as claims to Medicare. Commercial payers also collect data on patients and will continue to analyze the health of the population, the efficacy of treatments, and the rationale for tests and drugs. The outcome from analyzing this data will be more evidence-based treatments, and more predictions about an individual's health and the cost of maintaining them in a healthy state.

The collection and analysis of data will identify the lowest-cost providers compared with the highest achievement of quality. Providers will receive payments based on this data. There will be pressure to conform to evidence-based medicine, and those who comply will receive rewards while those who do not comply will incur penalties.

In addition, duplicate and unnecessary tests, and useless treatments are easily identified through the use of data analytics. Government research has also identified fraud through the use of analytics. The rate of prosecution and the recovery of payments escalated at the same time. Moreover, the government estimates that $80 billion are misspent every year on care.

In addition to narrow panels of providers on insurance plans, more consolidation of providers in networks will occur through ACOs. These organizations, tasked with improving and maintaining population health, can network and work together as members of an entity. In the past, the Federal Trade Commission (FTC) restricted organizations from getting too large in any marketplace in order to increase competition and keep prices down. The new focus on collaboration among providers created a need for change in this area.

Commercial insurers who joined the healthcare insurance exchange narrowed their list of providers. They narrowed it for two reasons. They could look at the performance of providers in order to choose those who achieved good outcomes at lower costs. Insurers can control what happens with a narrow network. They can also use analytics to test compliance with evidence-based treatment protocols.

Organizations such as Group Health (2014) have already initiated chronic care models into their practice plans. Group Health noted that "recent data show that more than 145 million people, or almost half of all Americans, live with a chronic condition. That number is projected to increase by more than one percent per year by 2030, resulting in an estimated chronically ill population of 171 million." This trend will continue as the focus on individual costs and low-cost treatment opportunities continue as a focus.

Insurers have added alternative medicine to their plans. They now cover acupuncture and other alternative treatments from Eastern medicine. As individuals pay more out-of-pocket, they also look for alternative and more natural ways of creating a healthy lifestyle that is less dependent on drugs. This trend will continue as individuals take more responsibility for their care. Providers call this acceptance "patient engagement," and they continue to explore more ways to engage the patient.

In the past, patients equated the quality of a physician office visit in terms of whether or not they left with a prescription in hand. Whether it was pain medication, an antibiotic, or some other medication targeted at the complaint they provided to the physician, they expected a prescription. All medications precipitate untoward effects; physicians did not highlight them, and patients did not ask about them. Most drugs are metabolized in the liver or the kidney. Now we have a generation of patients needing dialysis or transplant due to the overuse of medication.

> "In 2011, according to a survey by the Kaiser Family Foundation, Americans younger than 18 obtained an average of 4.1 prescriptions from retail pharmacies; those ages 19 to 64 filled an average of 11.9; and those older than 65 filled an average of 28. The Centers for Disease Control and Prevention reports that:

- In 2010, overdoses were the leading cause of injury death in the United States.
- Overdose death rates rose 102 percent between 1999 and 2010.
- Of the 38,329 overdose deaths in 2010, 60 percent involved pharmaceuticals.
- Of those deaths, approximately 75 percent were attributed to opioids and about 30 percent to benzodiazepines.
- One-third of all deaths from prescription painkillers are attributed to methadone, which originally was developed to help wean addicts off heroin. In 2011, misuse of drugs led to 2.5 million emergency department visits, of which 1.4 million were associated with pharmaceuticals." (Friedman, 2014).

The trend now is away from the overuse of antibiotics, which just helped bacteria evolve into tougher strains. People asked for sleep aids instead of exercising to become naturally tired or using meditation to relax. Now, physicians monitor their activities. Surgery was a common treatment for back pain, yet yoga, stretching, and massage often provided more benefit. In fact, Life in Yoga has trained 145 doctors, and its programs are recognized by the Accreditation Council for Continuing Medical Education (Rao, 2014).

In the 1990s, spine surgeons implanted rods, plates, and screws to strengthen the back, only to have patients complain after surgery that the pain from these implants was worse than the pain from their original complaint. Primary care physicians are now prescribing yoga, stretching exercises, and massage, and finding that the outcomes are better than surgery.

The field of genomics also persists as an important part of healthcare. Using data, early intervention can occur for individuals born or predisposed to certain conditions. This early intervention both increases the quality of life for these individuals and costs insurers less over the life of the individual. Targeted interventions use DNA typing of tumors to identify specific drug treatments. In the past, chemotherapy was based on a scatter-gun approach. Now, the treatment can be specific to the type of DNA in a tumor. The genomics of virus treatments are also moving in the same direction.

Along with the use of data for predictive analysis and retrospective evaluation, the digital revolution includes new ways of making better use of physician time. Limited specialists can see more patients through the use of telemedicine where they diagnose and advise local physicians on treatment plans and interventions, which maximizes the use of their expertise. Physician extender (physician assistants and nurse practitioners) ranks will continue to grow. They can safely treat chronic conditions while physicians diagnose and treat new patient conditions.

Summary

The future is the great unknown. However, healthcare is a sector that will continue to grow with an aging population. It is impossible to cover every business type and predict every trend or happening. Innovation will continue within the healthcare sector, and our hope is that it will begin to reach down to the individual and be rewarded and recognized.

Predictions, however, are open to the test of time. Future editions, if possible, will provide a scorecard on the accuracy and timeliness of these predictions as the healthcare sector continues to grow. The future is full of great opportunities, and possible failures from those who do not learn from the past. The healthcare sector will experience innovations that no one has yet conceived, as well as innovations to ensure that patients and employees are satisfied. Healthcare is going to be the responsibility of all participants and with that an overwhelming opportunity for innovation and the individual.

Discussion Questions

1. What kinds of innovation do you see in the care of patients? Describe innovations that are not gadget related. Instead, describe innovations in providing the care.
2. Assess the changes precipitated and regulated by the PPACA. Explain how they affect population health.
3. Justify the changes in healthcare provider and allied team member roles. Identify how innovation made these changes possible.

Assignment

Choose an innovation in healthcare delivery. Describe what precipitated this innovation. What role changes occurred? Describe the process for innovation. Predict future changes derived from this innovation. What role did leadership play in the development of this innovation? Support your evaluation and predictions.

Chapter 9

Leadership in Innovation

Introduction

Implementing innovation as a strategic venture for the organization requires supportive leadership. A supportive leader is one who not only ensures continued support both financially and strategically, but also ensures the availability of resources throughout the life of the project. The previous sentence appears easy to accomplish but, in reality, it has become a stumbling block for sustained innovation throughout the organization; because of changing priorities, competitive pressures, and a desire for cost efficiency, support from leadership could dissolve if conditions warrant a drastic change. A reality of this sector is that innovation is more relational in nature, and more open to power relationships and interests (Van Wijngaarden, et al. 2012). Support from leadership can often turn on a dime. Given these dynamic conditions, leadership of innovation is necessary to sort out the vision and embrace the priorities. This chapter describes the characteristics, strategy, and personal commitment needed for sustained success.

Leadership Characteristics

There exists a multitude of research efforts on the characteristics and traits of successful leaders. These characteristics are both innate and learned. Leaders who possess these characteristics will succeed more often in executing innovative outcomes to reach project completion.

The question that many have asked is whether a leader can be born or groomed into a specific position. Either way, leaders must possess certain characteristics:

1. Vision: Must have a definitive vision for the organization within the context of the industry. That vision must be shared and communicated.
2. Critical thinking skills: Leaders must possess the ability to reason, decide, and act in a manner that benefits the organization. Critical thinking requires an exceptional understanding of the business, and an innate sense of the past, present, and future. Leaders must be able to look inward, to accept one's lesser traits.
3. Communication skills: Leaders must be able to communicate across the organization. Communication does not mean delegation. Leaders must communicate their vision, values, and directives in clear and unambiguous language. Again, this seems much easier to discuss than to accomplish. Accept feedback and recommendations; the CEO and the support team's pronouncements and proclamations must align with the mission and purpose of the organization. In addition, senior management needs to solicit feedback from employees so that the message is both fully coordinated and integrated.
4. Empathy/trust: Leaders must have the ability to place themselves under the conditions and environment of another person or persons. Leaders must be able to understand how and why people behave as they do. That

is, leaders must be able to empathize with their employees. Leaders must trust their subordinates to perform.

5. Allocate sufficient resources: While verbal support is needed for affirmation of encouragement, resources are needed for project continuance. The senior manager that both supports and supplies resources to the project and provides the necessary continuity of support for the project.

6. Accountability: This is probably the most difficult aspect of being a leader within an organization. Accountability requires that the leader be able and willing to accept both the accolades of success and the responsibility of failure. This characteristic demands the most of a person and truly challenges their ethical and moral character.

Leadership, then, is a combination of both innate and learned abilities. Leadership is more about the person him(her)self than it is about the actual position. Leadership alone is insufficient for sustained innovation success.

Innovation and Leadership

"Leaders cast long shadows" (Robinson and Goudy, 2009). Their actions and behaviors are noticed by employees. For professionals (which encompasses much of this sector), performance is as much a factor of knowing what to do, as how to do it, and why it is important.

For innovation to succeed, it requires leadership and action. Leadership is a call to action—action that is planned and implemented with sufficient checks and balances. Therefore, the leader who intends to implement innovation in a strategic manner must first evaluate the organization and its readiness for innovation. Once the organization is ready, then they develop the strategy and, finally, implement the process.

Evaluating the Organization

Evaluation relies on empirical evidence. The leader must ensure that critical evidence concerning such items as operational flow, employee morale, organizational objectives, strategic plans, chain-of-command directives, and communications are correctly evaluated. Evaluation could also be synonymous with readiness for implementation. Surveys and interviews are viable methods to collect information on the organization's perceptions and attitudes. That is, management might present a survey or create a focus group to determine the readiness for implementation. A survey would provide a much fairer representation but the focus group would be much simpler and easier to administer. Focus groups usually consist of anywhere between twenty and fifty people gathered in one room who have agreed to participate in the discussions and offer their opinions, feelings, and beliefs regarding a particular topic, product, or service.

The choice of question and/or measurement is critical for evaluating the organization. Some typical questions for a focus group would include the following:

1. Describe how important concerns or critical information is communicated throughout the organization.
2. How would you assess the efficiency and effectiveness of the organization?
3. How would you assess employee morale in your organization?
4. Do organizational directives flow naturally from senior management staff?
5. Can you describe, in your own words, the mission of the organization?
6. Has innovation, in the past, been viewed positively?
7. Have previous innovation efforts been recognized throughout the organization or just within a department or function in which the innovation was implemented?

8. Do organizational strategies stress the need for innovation?
9. Irrespective of personality, does senior management willingly want innovation as part of their strategic objectives?
10. If you could rate how well the organization adopts an innovation culture on a scale of 1 to 10, with 1 being not ready to 10 being fully ready, which value would you assign to your organization?

Survey questions are more useful for specifics on topic issues. Gather data that is trustworthy, not only supportive. Look for inconsistencies, attempting to interpret the meaning of the information. The purpose is to give senior management an evaluation of the organization's responsiveness to a proposed change.

Once the first evaluation is complete, initiate plans for a yearly or bi-yearly evaluation. In the "Age of Information," it is difficult to understand why corporate communications are not fully involved in value feedback—from employees, shareholders, *and* customers. Take the "pulse" of the organization at regular intervals. Create metrics for management and scorecards to track progress.

Assessing the Readiness

Similar to the previous section, once the organization is evaluated, then readiness can be determined. *Readiness* is a term that indicates the acceptance of change and the resources needed to incorporate the change.

Acceptance of change refers to the ability of individuals to grasp, understand, and align with the change. When change takes place, people need to adjust, align, and adapt.

- Change can be painful or pleasing, depending on the situation and the people involved.
- Acceptance of change is a measure of acquiescence—accepting the change as permanent by

Statement Number	Instructions: Check the box that best matches your agreement (disagreement) with each statement	Strongly Disagree	Disagree	Neither Disagree nor Agree	Agree	Strongly Agree
1	When change occurs, I am one of the first to embrace it					
2	When my company announces a change, I believe it will be positive					
3	The outcomes of change are generally positive					
4	My organization does not create barriers to change					
5	People who embrace change quickly are better adjusted					
6	Change can be positive when barriers are reduced					
7	I would accept change if there were additional opportunities					
8	Accepting change can be made easier if management communicates					
9	If change reduces stress and anxiety, I would accept it					
10	There is never a feeling of loss associated with change					

Figure 9.1 Acceptance of change survey.

- Minimizing obstacles and barriers
- Developing opportunities for growth
- Developing a new "role" for employees
- Minimizing fear, anxiety, and a feeling of loss

A survey was created to measure acceptance of a change (see Figure 9.1). To complete the survey, assign a numerical value as follows: 1 = strongly disagree, 2 = disagree, 3 = neither disagree nor agree, 4 = agree, 5 = strongly agree.

- Calculate an average of the ten responses; expect averages to be close to 3.0.
- For each individual's average score < 3.0, have problems adjusting to change.
- For each individual's average score > 4.0, accepts change.

Note: Do not read into the responses more than the ability to assess how change is accepted.

- Examine the range for each individual's overall score; high variation indicates poor agreement between individual responses.

This suggests that change has been an upheaval for individuals with both positive and negative experiences. This person will accept change slowly, given the success (failure) experienced over time. They need alignment and adaptation time for the change to succeed.

The survey results provide information on the efficiency with which the change (a cross-functional innovation strategy) can occur. Individuals having problems with change or those who vary in responding across the ten statements will need more time to adjust. Of course, customers (patients) and suppliers could easily fit into these categories as well. For these stakeholders, a focus group session should prove beneficial (provide the survey and solicit questions from the group on the planned change).

Given the rapid changes occurring in the healthcare profession, organizations need to accept the challenge and identify those responsible for implementing these changes. Determine or assess if employees, contractors, and/or patients are ready for innovation (one of many changes). It is the responsibility of leadership to provide a manageable process of introducing, maintaining, and encouraging innovations into the organization. If employees, customers (patients), and/or stakeholders experience the benefits of continuous innovation, there will be little reason to return or desire the existing paradigm. Consider the 3M Corporation, a recognized leader in innovation, which developed an effective corporate innovation strategy that balanced costs with the needs of people (Thomke, 2002).

Developing a Strategy for a Healthcare Organization

"In an organization undergoing seismic change, today's healthcare executive is entitled to feel a little shell shocked. Technologies are evolving at light speed, yielding an expectation for enhanced mobility, collaboration, and access to information. Breakthroughs in treatment modalities, therapeutic options, and patient care seem to be reported every week" (Robinson and

Goudy, 2009). The change at times must feel like an upheaval. The healthcare leader must deal with changing priorities, changing technology, and a changing and dynamic workforce. For the healthcare sector, there are three realities that leadership must prepare the organization to encounter: (1) prepare for current and future realities, (2) engage stakeholders to fully participate in the process, and (3) focus on tangible and consistent business results (Robinson and Goudy, 2009). Leaders provide the strategy that motivates the organization to accept change.

Developing a strategy requires an understanding of how this strategy will be accepted and implemented throughout the organization. According to Fleuren, Wiefferink, and Paulussen (2004), there are four main stages of the innovation process, from a strategic perspective:

1. Dissemination
2. Adoption
3. Implementation
4. Sustainment (continuance)

Transitioning from one stage to the next is affected by various determinants, divided into specific characteristics:

■ Characteristics of the socio-political context, such as rules, legislation, and patient characteristics
■ Characteristics of the organization, such as staff turnover or the decision-making process in the organization
■ Characteristics of the person adopting the innovations (user of the innovation), such as knowledge, skills, and perceived support from colleagues
■ Characteristics of the innovation, such as complexity or relative advantage (Fleuren, Wiefferink, and Paulussen, 2004, p, 108)

The organization incorporates innovation into a strategy, given the frequency of "game-changing" event(s). It moves the process because the environment dictates such changes. It may be slow or fast; the driver is activity that demands change. Considering the dynamic and changing nature of the healthcare business, the stimulus to innovate exists.

Developing and implementing an innovation strategy requires order, consistency, and stability. It is a difficult task for leadership and it depends on risk aversion. Even more so because many believe that innovatoin is solely synonymous with invention. Inventions or discoveries are discrete events; they happen by chance. These are difficult to plan for, not knowing if the discovery will have commercial or lasting value. The strategy discussed in this section is for planned innovations to maintain sustained competitive or brand advantage.

Developing a strategy that enables innovation to occur in any function or department requires the following:

1. Acceptance that the innovation begins and ends with the individual (employee, patient, supplier, etc.)
2. Collecting needs for evaluation (viability, capability, sustainability)
3. A methodology for evaluating potential innovation projects (using the ENOVALE™ framework)
4. Defined benefits
5. Linkages to financial or organizational goals
6. Decision-making criteria for acceptance or rejection

Rather than reinvent the wheel, management (i.e., leadership) can use the ENOVALE framework as a viable methodology. This permits the organization to design a strategy that is unique to its specific needs. Designing such a corporate-wide innovation strategy requires

- Strategic objectives (what the innovation will accomplish)
- SWOT analysis (Strengths, Weaknesses, Opportunities, Threats)
- Organization culture open to innovation (this can be developed over time)

■ A logical process for implementation
■ Responsive communications
■ Efficient decision-making processes
■ Validation
■ Verification

Healthcare poses a diversity of products, services, and technologies. Strategies employed at a medical products facility will be very different from those at a healthcare facility. The scale of the implementation will also be very different. For the healthcare facility, innovations would be more improvement or change oriented, require far less processing, and be far more patient focused. On the other hand, for medical products companies, a comprehensive strategy requires more processing, a longer implementation time, and involves fewer individuals.

The purpose here is not to develop a generic strategy, as this would not have applicability to anyone, but rather to discuss what is needed to begin the strategic process—in essence, the introductory essentials needed to develop the strategy. Smaller facilities and businesses can develop a simpler strategy (Figure 9.2) without a rigid process wherein only the key elements of ENOVALE are used to facilitate facility-wide innovation.

An innovative workforce and organization can maintain brand status (competitive advantage), a higher efficiency, and a more motivated workforce. The benefits far outweigh the cost, time, and resources of implementation.

Implementing the Strategy

The most difficult element as this begins is the commitment of personnel, resources, and funding from the organization to this philosophy. Leadership is most critical at this stage—and most challenged at this stage. Implementing innovation requires that the four stages that precede this stage are complete.

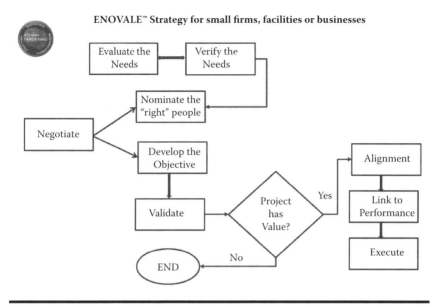

ENOVALE™ Strategy for small firms, facilities or businesses

Figure 9.2 ENOVALE™ strategy for small businesses, firms, and facilities.

Leaders and managers must prepare the organization for this type of innovation. They must prepare a strategy that

1. Incorporates innovation as a strategic goal for all departments and functions, including the number of projects, realized benefits, and needed resources
2. Creates a 1- to 2-year plan for operationalizing innovation within all departments
3. Establishes baseline metrics (applicable to different departments)
4. Establishes a scorecard approach to track progress
5. Identifies personnel and resources
6. Assigns a functional or departmental leader who is responsible for success
7. These unfulfilled needs should drive organizations to develop products, services, and technology to meet these wants and desires

Strategies must never be rigid. The strategy provides a baseline from which to build innovation throughout the organization.

Given the differences between businesses in the healthcare sector, we cannot state a specific strategy that will work for all organizations. Each strategy is tailored to the organization. However, we can state that the ENOVALE framework is applicable to both large and small businesses alike. The actual strategy must be directed to the needs of the organization, and its patients, customers, and stakeholders.

As much as different organizations generate a unique strategy, so too does a strategy for an internal function or department within an organization. Departmental objectives vary by job responsibility and purpose. Some departments are more operational, others more administrative, and others more intangible (services). Each is unique, and each has a strategy that can include innovation as a daily activity.

Corporate (Administrative) versus Functional (Departmental) Strategies

Once a corporate strategy or organizational strategy is developed and implemented, each function should follow on with a scaled plan that meets all corporate and functional objectives. The strategy to implement innovation in Human Resources (HR) is very different in scope and intent from that developed for financial functions. The objectives, metrics, and time frames will vary but the approach and methods will be similar.

In the past, innovations (inventions and discoveries) could be easily measured as a tangible item. Costing processes, resources allocated, and project management permitted tracking and evaluation. However, with a functional or departmental approach, these obvious measures of performance do not yet exist or have not been used for such purposes. Either the organization or business can devise a new scheme, or they can use what is available.

It is important to note here that not all internal innovation projects will produce vast savings, reduced costs, or secure competitive advantage. On the one hand, many innovation projects will yield significant intangible benefits (motivation, improve communications, better usage of time). Although it is not difficult to realize that a more efficient, more motivated, and better communicating staff is truly competitive, these intangible innovations are clearly visible in the healthcare sector and often patient focused.

Leadership and ENOVALE

A natural next step is to examine the ENOVALE method in terms of leadership support, engagement, and as a methodology for implementing innovation management throughout an organization. Examining the detailed ENOVALE structure permits an evaluation of how leadership interacts with the methodological approach. Beyond the role of leadership in establishing a strategy, it also contributes to process rollout and sustains the project, and is involved in all critical decision making, including whether the project moves to the implementation stage.

Table 9.1 demonstrates the need for leadership (management) to stay involved with the innovation process. Failure to connect will result in long-term problems, missed opportunities, and inconsistent decision making. Following the ENOVALE process includes a number of entry and exit points for management (leadership). These decision points are not burdensome; decisions are made based on empirical evidence. Success depends not only on the culture that exists, but also on the process utilized and the strategy applied.

Table 9.1 Compatibility of Leadership Characteristics and ENOVALE Elements

ENOVALE Step	Critical Elements	Leader Characteristics	Strategic
1	Open ideas	Critical thinking	Yes
	Needs assessment	Accountability	Yes
	Internal	Communication	Yes
	External	Communication	Yes
	Needs evaluation	Accountability	Yes
	Requirements	Critical thinking	Yes
	User	Critical thinking	Yes
	Functional	Critical thinking	Yes
2	Team composition	Allocate resources	No
	Select by innovation type	Trust	No
	Values recognition	Vision/ Communication	Yes
	Environment scan	Critical thinking	Yes
	Understanding of innovation	Critical thinking	Yes
	Alignment of purpose	Vision/ Communication	Yes
3	Develop objectives	Values/ Communication	Yes
	Evaluate SMART criteria	Critical thinking	No
	Sync with requirements	Accountability	Yes
	Create outcomes	Resource allocation	No

Table 9.1 (continued)   Compatibility of Leadership Characteristics and ENOVALE Elements

ENOVALE Step	Critical Elements	Leader Characteristics	Strategic
4	Requirements/ Objectives	Accountability	Yes
	Limitations	Resource allocation	Yes
	Assumptions	Resource allocation	Yes
	Success/Risk—SREM	Critical thinking	Yes
	Validated outcomes	Accountability	Yes
5	Alignment	Vision/ Communication	Yes
	Assess values	Accountability	No
	Assess expectations	Vision/ Communication	No
	Project team aligned	Empathy/Trust	No
6	Link to performance	Resource allocation	Yes
	Metrics	Critical thinking	Yes
	Financial	Vision/ Accountability	Yes
	Project	Vision/ Accountability	Yes
	Human	Empathy/ Accountability	Yes
7	Evaluate	Accountability	Yes
	Execute	Accountability	Yes

Innovation Culture

For an innovative culture to become established, leadership may need to reinvent itself to support and commit to this new reality. At present, different cultures or spheres of influence exist within the organization. Examining these different types of cultural spheres of influence (networks) operating within the organization reveals how management and leadership interact in a high-tech innovative culture.

Spheres of influence or networks are cultural phenomena. They operate adjacent to the prevailing organization culture. They can also be thought of as "personal and professional networks" (P&P networks). They exist between individuals with like-minded goals, backgrounds, and functional assignments. Figure 9.3 represents an overall consensus of P&P networks with regard to innovation. P&P networks are defined as personal and intra-personal communication and work linkages.

In fact, these networks can be considered subcultures within the organization. They have a complete social, work,

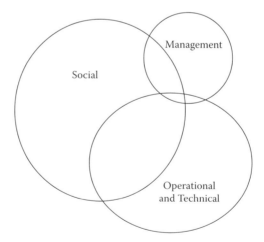

Figure 9.3   Conceptual diagram of social networks operating in high-tech companies. (Adapted from Figure 4.1 in McLaughlin 1995, *Total Quality in Research and Development*. Delray Beach, FL: St. Lucie Press, p. 96.)

and functional dimension. Employees in these networks align well with each other, share common goals and practices, and consider each other peers. These networks exist in highly technical organizations with extensive expenditures in Research & Development. For the healthcare sector, these are the large pharmaceutical, medical products, and bio-tech firms.

The largest circle is the social dimension. People in this subculture search for like-minded individuals who share common goals on a social or daily basis. These individuals often create their own lingo and phrasing to identify themselves. In addition, this dimension represents social relationships, friendships, natural teams, and individuals empathetic to one another. Remember that this subculture is built around innovation strategy, activities, and projects in the organization.

The second subculture is technical and operational—this is how employees operate on a more professional basis. Like individuals share common goals and objectives, and readily align with each other. Individuals who belong to related professional societies understand this unique subculture; for example, technical, engineering, and scientific personnel align with each other in this subculture.

The third subculture is management, which only interacts marginally with the other subcultures. Managers align with others in similar positions. For innovation, management generally operates outside of decision making and resource allocation. There is little interaction with either of the other subcultures, and this is why the groups often seem disconnected. The lack of interaction is not intentional, but programmed. Most management takes a "hands-off" approach to innovation.

Examining Figure 9.3 reveals that management generally interacts little with the existing innovation culture. Management evaluates the project and makes a decision to accept or reject. Leadership, on the other hand, must take a more proactive role with innovation, changing or realigning the underlying social (cultural) basis in which innovation operates.

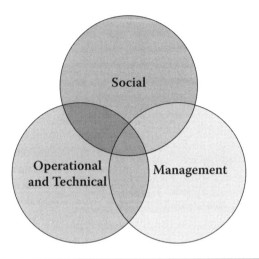

Figure 9.4   Rebalanced innovation subculture.

In the realigned (rebalanced) system (Figure 9.4), there is a confluence of all subcultures where innovation is a concern. Innovation is one strategy that all can align with and leadership can use to achieve sustained competitive advantage. Innovation is both an end goal and a strategy. It has both leadership and operational components. "Innovation and creativity are the results of an open, secure, interactive environment where knowledge is readily available. Innovation comes from the individual when needs are met and the mind is free to explore the universe of possibilities" (McLaughlin, 1995, p. 101). What was said 20 years ago readily applies today.

A management system that promotes a culture of innovation will exhibit six characteristics:

1. Reduce fear and anxiety.
2. Establish a strong sense of values and ethical principles.
3. Work toward achievable goals for innovation.
4. Accept failure and learn from it.
5. Remove unwarranted risks.
6. Reward commensurate with individuals and teams.

Innovation should be a "natural" for a leader as it is one way to achieve competitive advantage. Again, taking a "hands-off" approach may work well for the leader/manager but the ramifications can be destructive in the long run. Too many useful innovation projects were discarded because management delegated the decision to those without a wide stakeholder view. There is a time for intervention and a time for restraint. Let subordinates know the rules and when management involvement will occur. With ENOVALE, it was easy to identify when management was or was not influential. As head and director of the management system, the leader can help mold the organization into one that is accepting of innovation.

Going Forward

Leadership is one critical component of sustained innovation success in healthcare. Without this vital component, the innovation would languish waiting for approvals. Someone must make a decision to move the project forward. Without specific direction, innovations would be happenstance, limited to a group or function. The healthcare sector leader going forward will need

1. Courage—to lead rather than follow; manage the rumor mill
2. Bravery—create an environment that reduces personal risk, allows mistakes, accept the feedback from others even when it counteracts the leaders thinking
3. Accommodating - work well with others; stand your ground only when sound reasoning suggests no change
4. Be responsible—to peers, subordinates, employees, patients, and stakeholders

The challenge is real but the rewards are substantial for the business!

Summary

This chapter discussed the need for leadership in innovation. The leader plays a vital role in developing, supporting, managing, and guiding the innovation effort within an organization or business. Leaders are generally not born but are, in fact, developed. Leadership for innovation success entails not only the individual, but also his or her leadership style, values, ethics, and experiences. Leadership for innovation requires courage, accountability, and the ability to interject oneself into the innovation project when needed. The leader provides fundamental support and guidance, becoming the decision maker and final judge. The leader develops, with his peers, the strategy of innovation and then implements that innovation strategy for overall sustained success. Without leadership's influence and support, innovation on a sustained basis would fail.

Discussion Questions

1. Discuss what it means to be a leader. Identify five characteristics and link each characteristic to some element of innovation.
2. Discuss the steps needed to develop a strategy for your organization (or a hypothetical organization) for sustained innovation success.
3. What are the unique problems with leading innovation in the healthcare sector? Consider items such as changing policies, frequent new technologies, brand recognition versus competitive advantage, professionalism, the role of the physician, etc.
4. If you are or would aspire to be the leader of a healthcare organization, what three practices would you use to ensure sustained success?

5. How does strong leadership avert problems such as high employee turnover, organizational loyalty, demotivated employees, dissatisfied patients, angry regulators, etc.?

Assignments

1. Write a short job description (no more than one paragraph containing five to eight sentences) that describes the role of a leader in an innovative organization. Include specifics about the healthcare sector that the leader would operate within. Be sure to highlight characteristics that are needed, not just for job performance, but for overall success.
2. What problems do leaders encounter when implementing innovation in a healthcare setting? Be specific as to the problems and pose a solution to each problem. Finally, assign a ranking to the problem/solution being implemented in your or another organization/business.
3. Which of the ENOVALE steps do you believe would be most difficult for leadership? What actions could be taken to avert this reaction?

Chapter 10

Innovation and the Individual

Introduction

One explicit finding of our research shows that innovation begins and ends with the individual. The individual is the innovator or the recipient of innovation through scanning the environment for unsatisfied needs, wants, or desires. Individuals, with maturity, acquire experience with products, services, and technologies. They know what works well, what needs improvement, and when a change is required. Their acquired knowledge and experience are used to judge innovation and—consequently—changing (or continuing) purchase behaviors. If an item meets a new or unsatisfied need and the item offers better, lasting, or additional performance, then that item is judged as innovative.

The Individual as Judge and Jury

Does the manufacturer, producer, or creator know best if something is innovative? Of course with proper research and analytics, the answer is yes when the product is new and original. However, even the newest products, services, or technologies may not resonate with the public (individuals). This lack of acceptance indicates that a need remains unsatisfied, or that the performance is not quite better than existing like items. Therefore, the individual is the lynchpin in innovation assessment as well as the evaluator of the feasibility of the item.

How and why individuals assess an item as innovative or not innovative truly depends on their experience, their expectations, and their knowledge. Recall Figure 3.4 from Chapter 3; this model serves as the basis for Global Targeting's unique approach to innovation. The right-hand portion of the model represents the organization's plan to create an innovative outcome, while the left-hand portion represents the process each individual uses to evaluate whether or not the innovative outcome is innovation. Figure 10.1 is a "slice" of the model in which the individual participates.

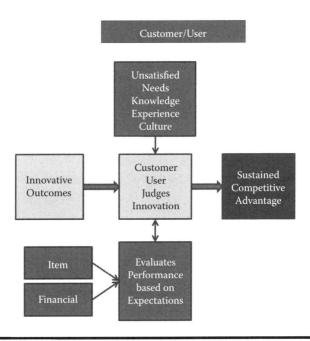

Figure 10.1 Individual's process of evaluating innovation. (Adapted from McLaughlin, G. and Caraballo, V., *ENOVALE: How to Unlock Innovation Project Success,* Taylor & Francis, Boca Raton, FL, 2013b.)

The healthcare sector is unique in that the output is judged from competitive advantage to patient satisfaction. The innovative outcome is a measure of success, as innovation is judged using experience, knowledge, and performance. Innovation in this sector runs the gambit from new discoveries to highly intangible services.

Individuals do not use a standardized evaluation method for innovation. This disparity identifies why McLaughlin and Caraballo (2013b) discuss innovation focused on how it is experienced, as either new, improved, or changed. Patients' judgment is based on knowledge, experience, culture, and needs. Performance enters the evaluation with experience and knowledge. Before making a purchase or value decision, the individual must assess financial concerns. Discussing each element in detail provides a better understanding of how critical the individual is to innovation.

Unsatisfied Needs: Individual Perspective

If patients need something to make them comfortable, this need becomes a driving concern that, until satisfied, is paramount. Satisfying that need is not innovative in itself, but it does benefit the business or organization. Benefits to the organization could be the distinguishing characteristic that patients/customers respond to and respect. Satisfying simple needs is a powerful objective: it can literally predict fortune or failure. Identifying and understanding these needs becomes a strategic imperative.

Often, patient (or customer) satisfaction surveys collect "after-the-fact" information that provides limited value. Satisfaction is a momentary feeling but, over time and with experience, it attains permanency. Like innovation, knowledge and experience establish satisfaction paradigms (beliefs) that are difficult to displace. Satisfaction surveys, if designed properly, can provide valuable information on needs (both unsatisfied and future). Otherwise, the information offers limited value for either correcting problems or predicting future behaviors. This constraint seems the case for most satisfaction surveys reviewed by the authors (McLaughlin and Richins). When the need becomes a collective request, then it creates the opportunity for innovation. The organization offering the product, service, or technology must recognize these collective needs. These needs are both transitory and permanent— transitory needs in the sense that alternative products, services, or technologies may fill a short-term need. For the uncomfortable patient who receives assistance, the need is met until the next incidence. Not meeting this perceived need permanently results in continuous dissatisfaction. Innovation is never defined when the need is transitory. Over time, many transitory needs become permanent. Therefore, a collection of critical information on these needs must be an organizational strategic objective.

As an example, a survey conducted by Health Information Management Systems Society (HIMSS) identified new mobile opportunities. "The most frequently identified barrier to the use of mobile technology is the lack of funding; this fact was identified by 71 percent of respondents" (HIMSS Mobile Technology Survey, 2014). They also noted immaturity in the marketplace. However, both providers and patients continue to look for apps that help them manage healthcare needs. The technology is fascinating to some, a necessity to others, and to the rest an inconvenience at best. People search for the best solutions, especially when it is in their best interest. If the need drives action, then action it will be until the future changes the need. More simply, people will strive to meet their unsatisfied needs.

Knowledge and Innovation

Knowledge of the product or likely substitute is critical for judging innovation. Acquisition of the knowledge may come from many sources. Some are very reliable; others are unreliable. When patients describe the benefits of a new drug to another person, most of the time they do not provide a list of precautionary items. The information is partially correct, but not 100% perfect. Individuals filter information for their own specific needs.

Knowledge is a combination (usually unequal) of information and experience. Individuals take in information from many sources, filtering out what is unimportant. Filtering of different media will result in a very different knowledge perspective. If someone advertises a product as innovative, that person must first learn of the item and then evaluate the item from his or her experience. Advertising via television is a powerful medium. However, when informing a prospective buyer, the advertiser may provide information that is not pertinent or not yet validated. A suggestion that an item is innovative may be true or not, depending on whether the receiver of the information validates that claim. Individuals validate the claim of innovation through knowledge acquired and the performance expected and observed (Figure 10.2). A good example is the use of advertising to educate patients about the drugs available to treat their specific healthcare needs. Most men would not know or question whether they have

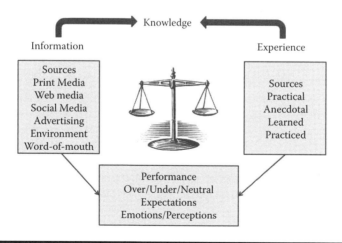

Figure 10.2   Knowledge link to performance.

low testosterone levels. However, advertising brings attention to such a possibility, and the patient brings up the topic
during a visit to the physician and leaves with a prescription
to raise his testosterone level. The media directs information
to a very select group, especially if the innovation is outside
normal parameters. The message can be direct, subtle, or
implied, depending on the item itself. For the low testosterone
example, although the user may be a man, a woman may be
the prime purchaser, so the message must be persuasive to the
purchaser as well as meet an unsatisfied need.

The medium or method of accepting the message is as critical as the experience one has with the item. Interest piques
when an item meets an unsatisfied need. Interest generates
further information gathering. Patients use services such as
WebMD® to help diagnose ailments before seeking a physician's advice. This search for information was used to meet a
need. What the patient may lack is experience with the illness'
symptoms, complications, interactions, and duration (this could
be a measure of performance). With experience, the patient
knows (in general) what to expect and generally requires little
or no information.

A good example of finding the best practice was shared by
a couple who had a daughter with club foot. The surgeon told
them that the child needed multiple surgeries over the course
of her childhood. Instead, the couple found a little-used (but
successful since 1955) treatment that corrected the problem
using casts instead of surgery. They opted for this solution
and, at age 6, their daughter walks normally and no one
would ever know she was born with club foot (Gold, 2014).

A patient (customer) will search for alternatives when the
need arises. In fact, the person may search for an alternative if
something about the existing product, service, or technology
disturbs or upsets them. When information is readily available,
as it is with the Internet, individuals may search for information to confirm or reassure themselves, especially when the
need is critical. Understanding the needs of customers and

patients is critical for developing purchase, brand, or customer loyalty.

Experience

Experiences are learned behaviors and encounters over a
period of time with an object or item. Experiences can vary
from abundant to minimal. Those with a large amount of
experience can be focused and use these experiences solely
for decision making. Those with minimal experience often
superimpose substitutes as a means of evaluation. Subtle differences in substitutes, as compared with the original, can
affect the evaluation of the outcome. The greater the experience, the more useful the decision process is to the patient or
consumer. At times, experience will outweigh available information in judging innovation. Whether the individual judges
the product as innovative, a change in purchasing patterns, or
an increase in perceived value is a positive for the organization. Therefore, this perception is why achieving competitive
advantage (value) is the final element of the Global Targeting,
Inc. model (see Figure 10.1).

Emotions run parallel with experiences. Individuals will
purchase a new product (patients want the latest test) just for
the sake of something new. The logic described in Figure 10.1
is rejected for the pleasure obtained with any new purchase.
For most, this rejection is a rare occurrence, and more thought
and evaluation are given before a purchase is complete.
Emotions certainly influence—and are influenced by—the
needs of the individual.

Innovation operates in a similar manner. If the customer
(or patient) has an unsatisfied need and knowledge of the
product, service, or technology, he or she will use this knowledge (based on unequal parts of information and experience),
combined with an expectation of performance, to evaluate
innovation. Wellness or an expectation of good health is now
used by payers and providers to create patient loyalty; they

can send customized texts to patients that help the patients comply with their treatment plan. For example, during pregnancy, a text might say that it is time to schedule your sonogram or it is time to purchase a car seat. It is possible to provide information that helps patients make healthy decisions that vastly increase their quality of life. In contrast, a system to collect specific information on patient concerns, needs, or desires may provide valuable information to providers. The key is a two-way system of communications—both the information necessary to give to the patient and the information from the patient to make their experience.

The healthcare industry is finding that the more information a person can find, the more proficient that person will be at making an informed decision. The well-informed patient/customer is more discriminating in his or her selection, thus enabling the brand leader to experiment with the amount, content, and presentation of the information. The brand leader has a unique opportunity to both set the operational/functional requirements for the product/service/technology as well as limit potential competitors. By establishing dominance, the producer can create the standard by which all other alternatives are measured.

Information also confirms the experience of individuals, thus reducing the wait time for purchase. The opposite works in much the same manner. When experience is not confirmed or the experience has led to a different conclusion, the resulting action could be negative word-of-mouth, a purchase decision to use a competitor, or a change in healthcare provider.

Performance

Performance was discussed in Chapter 5. Expectations of performance (both real and imagined) are just as powerful. Knowledge brings both information and experience together to judge how well an item performs. If we expect an item to perform consistently, then any deviation will result in a loss of confidence. If expectations are exceeded, performance is judged favorably and may result in being identified as innovative. Performance takes on both tangible and intangible characteristics, and this is the reason for individual assessment. What may be innovative to one person may be status quo (or worse) to another. This disparity is one reason why innovation is not a universally held belief, as some would have their expectations be less than exemplary. Although Level 1 original designs have limited information and no experiential base, performance expectations can still exist.

1. Rather than trying to assume that providers know the patient, one should ask them to provide information on their stay or visit in regard to performance. Performance information can be general or specific. For patients, collect and evaluate general information on such items as wait times (especially those that deviate greatly from expectation).
2. Previous experiences.
3. Attitude of physicians, employees, and service staff.
4. Time spent with patient.
5. Registration and discharge procedures.
6. Patient interaction with doctors and nurses (Does the patient feel involved? Is their information respected?).
7. Adequacy/effectiveness of communications (Is the patient consulted? Treated with respect? Treated like an adult?)
8. Other pertinent issues, as required.

Performance issues are often overlooked, and yet they form the basis for experiences and expectations. Innovations are not recognized from an individual perspective without developed experiences. If brand loyalty is such an important issue to the healthcare sector, then measuring and tracking performance becomes paramount for judging innovation.

Culture

Cultural and ethnic issues do play a role in perceiving innovation but not to the degree or extent that most would expect. Project Impact Institute research continues to affirm that most cultures recognize the "New," Improved," and "Change" themes of innovation, although the order of importance may vary (McLaughlin and Caraballo, 2013a). This identification is critical for profit-focused businesses because knowing how to market an innovation is critical for sustained success. The idea of achieving competitive advantage comes not only from the product, service, or technology offered, but also from how it is presented to prospective buyers. For nonprofits, the "value" of the innovation to reduce cost, improve satisfaction, etc. is well understood among a diverse set of cultures evaluated to date.

As Project Impact collects and processes more cultural groups, the results may vary. To date, there is much conformity in the result that individuals can identify innovation beyond pure discovery or invention. However, recent data from Asia suggests that "new" innovation is easily identified, while improvement and change seem indistinguishable for the group overall. But when examining categorizations such as generations, younger groups use less experience to judge innovation while older groups rely on experience as a key determinant in identifying the three "means" of innovation. Older groups can experience innovation in all three forms.

In summary, Figure 10.1 is critical in understanding how the individual understands and evaluates innovation. What is innovative to one person may not be innovative to another. Individuals will not judge an item innovative with 100% certainty. However, when the criteria are met (Figure 10.1), the innovation will affect their purchase decisions, change their expectations, and establish a new standard of performance. With additional research, this relationship/interaction will likely become better understood and more predictable. Innovative healthcare organizations need to recognize that innovation cannot be claimed but must be experienced. "Walking the talk" is the best advertiser of innovation success. Selected projects, functioning in one department, suggest a special event process rather than an integrated approach. Multiple examples of innovation success operating in more than one department will provide validation. Organizations must focus their efforts on the group (or groups) that the innovation is meant to serve or be ready to modify both the message and response.

Purchase Behaviors (Value)

Studying the behavior of individuals (consumers/patients) is a field all of its own. What satisfies one may not satisfy another. This information is required if the largest percentage of patients is satisfied with an encounter. For example, the Hospital Consumer Assessment of Healthcare Providers and Systems (HCAHPS) requirements were determined by looking at patient satisfaction data collected by vendors and hospitals. The twenty-seven items were determined from experience with satisfaction surveys. Now these items are standard. Therefore, patients who receive more than the expected twenty-seven items in satisfaction will use word-of-mouth (or other means) to express their satisfaction. Healthcare facilities that offer exceptional patient value are innovative if an unsatisfied need is met. Whether it is labeled innovative or not, a true and lasting benefit can be sustained. Remember that the reason an organization innovates is to receive a sustained benefit; whether that be competitive advantage, or higher quality ratings, or something it truly values. A recent focus to improve scores is the implementation of patient navigators to assist patients in finding resources and ensuring coordination of care. This innovation will again become the standard of care because the Patient Protection and Affordable Care Act (PPACA) requires that patient navigators provide expertise on eligibility, enrollment, and coverage details for each health plan. They must share accurate information that is fair, impartial, and accurate. They are also tasked with facilitating enrollment in appropriate plans and assisting in conflict resolution between enrollees and their health plan.

Products, services, or technology with a label of "innovation" must strive to achieve all that the label entails. Advertisers may label their items as innovative—but the individual is the final judge. A change in purchasing decisions or a decision to use a different healthcare provider requires events and consequences that are either positive or negative. Innovation is one such event that will accomplish a paradigm change.

Figure 10.1 shows that innovation leads to competitive advantage. Competitive advantage is achieved through new purchase behaviors and sustained market share. Individuals purchase more of the product, service, or technology or experience greater value. The more often these events occur, the stronger the market position. When patients have a choice in selecting a healthcare facility, they first obtain personal recommendations, use media to learn about the facility, and compare the information provided to previous experiences. If the performance (a measure of service, efficiency, empathic staff, wait time, physician/nurse attitude, etc.) is better at the new facility, there is sufficient reason to move to the new facility. The patient will find it necessary to make the change and maintain a new relationship with the healthcare provider. Often value is achieved by offering an alternative that is too good to disregard.

The same is true of an organization not valuing its patients. Here, emotions play a role and perceptions can be changed with a poor experience. Values form the basis of what the person believes and acts upon. For nonprofits, value is the result of what innovation brings. Unlike satisfaction, which is temporary, values are permanent. If the patient values the experience at the physician's office or hospital outpatient facility, then that patient judges all experiences from this perspective. Capturing this information is critical for understanding how and what is judged innovative. The discussion is similar to that in measuring performance, that is, whether the organization uses a lagging or leading indicator. Satisfaction is a lagging indicator, and value is a leading indicator. Leading indicator information provides more "value" as it establishes baselines, a key element of effective metrics and dashboards. The process for gathering this information consists of surveys, interviews, and focus groups. However, this requires a paradigm change as most organizations collect lagging indicators more frequently.

If an individual detects a negative, she will react by expressing her dissatisfaction through complaints, actions, or word-of-mouth. If more than one individual expresses the same dissatisfaction, it becomes a call to action for the organization. Rather than searching for someone to blame, resources and energies should be used to correct the problem, thus reestablishing value. If the problem remains unsolved or, worse, unaddressed, the patient opts for a different venue, changing her paradigm.

Healthcare and the Individual

The notion of individual is clearly seen from a patient's perspective. Each patient's needs are different. Most are not searching for an innovative approach but, if encountered, would change their perspective. Yet healthcare must be innovative throughout its operations and administrations to profit from innovation. Considering only those Level 1 or 2 inventions as innovation greatly reduces the potential and benefit of this phenomenon. So often, this description of innovation prevents the "everyday" innovations from surfacing and serving patients and customers. Yes, some individuals implement their improvements without management support or agreement. Many, however, withhold their innovative ideas because the organization has demonstrated a lack of interest in these solutions or because no reward or recognition is possible.

Innovation ideas (needs) are not suggestions; therefore, do not try to treat them as such. If a process is instituted internally to collect ideas (needs), be sure that these are evaluated using the ENOVALE™ Solutions framework. To be most effective, a good communications, rewards, and recognition process must be in place. The best method is focus groups, surveys, and interviews—a structured process.

Not everyone is innovative at all times. At different times, some are much more innovative, some less so because the desire to innovate may vary over time or with interest. The Global Targeting Perceptions of Innovation survey (McLaughlin and Caraballo, 2013a) classifies individuals into one of the themed categories: New, Improved, or Change. If a person demonstrates a skill (a strength) in one of these three categories, then select such individuals when working a specific innovation type.

A competitive advantage comes from encouraging employees to contribute to future innovation efforts. It not only includes the obvious products or services, but also those that benefit internal operations and cross-department dialogue and cooperation. Reward and recognize the individual, as this is key to success. Employees are glad to contribute when the contribution is meaningful and recognized. Competition here is self-defeating, as it would be unfortunate to judge an idea before completing the vetting process. The idea/needs pair is competing for acceptance, not the employees. In fact, the best suggestions would be made incognito so that favoritism is not an issue. A computer program could keep the names and identities hidden until the project is approved.

Part of the process is informing (training) patients to offer suggestions, ideas, and needs as well as recognizing innovation when it occurs. Often, patients are provided with some form of orientation. Innovation could be part of that orientation. Briefing the patient or resident is a short process. Items could include

- Recognizing innovation and identifying the individual responsible
- Making suggestions based on needs
- Rewards and recognition for innovation ideas carried to completion
- How innovation benefits all

A simple introduction could ask patients to participate in the sustained improvement process.

   Training the individual (employee, provider, customer, and patient) is critical for sustained innovation. Much of the training can be subtle, as described above, or directed for employees and service providers. The availability of information over the Internet is giving rise to a more-informed, better-trained customer (patient). The informed person will want better treatment, request more information, and have higher expectations. Organizations that recognize this trend will want to become innovative so as to maintain their status as brand leaders with a loyal base.

A Collective Perspective

With the advent of big data/analytics, it is possible to better categorize individuals into common behavior groups. Data strategists are searching to identify like groups of individuals to better facilitate their unique needs. As innovation serves to meet needs, a major effort is underway to identify the characteristics of these groups so that more "individualized" marketing can be accomplished. Marketers will need to define numerous measures and characteristics that the group shares, for better alignment. Some of the common classification characteristics include

- Age
- Gender

- Position:
  - Years of experience
  - Experience
- Educational level:
  - Field of study
  - Certificates, certifications
- Salary level:
  - Disposable income
- Medical history:
  - Pharmaceutical use
  - Hospital stays (including emergency room visits)

Some of the more "individualized" characteristics include

- Color preference
- Favorite foods:
  - Restaurant patronage
- Technology orientation
- Past purchase history
- Shopping preferences

Not only would a data strategist examine these patterns, but he or she would also look for those who interacted and those who had little or nothing in common (Figure 10.3). Once categorized, individuals are assigned to like groups. Communications and print, electronic, and social media can then be precisely targeted. The same logic and reasoning can be applied to "selling" brand image, purchasing decisions, and innovation.

A very detailed analysis of the individual may reveal strikingly similar patterns. These patterns may coalesce into a description of a specific group of people all sharing very similar characteristics. This group or cluster forms a "centroid of information" identified for purposes of targeted marketing and sales. This same "centroid of information" could be targeted for medical, healthcare facility, or pharmaceutical purposes.

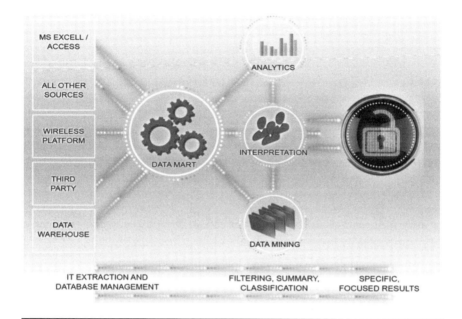

Figure 10.3   Data strategist function: unlocking focused data for decision making.

At first, a nonfocused approach is applied. This approach can be easily seen on television/Internet for patients with similar symptoms or those suffering from a named disease. However, the intensity and focus would be greater for this group.

Individuals hear or see information about a group similar to themselves that they would feel a natural affinity for. It would also be the message they need and want as it would focus on one or more unfulfilled needs. The individual would feel that the message was directed at them and that any purchase or participation would be beneficial to them. Ultimately, they could find others who think similar to themselves. For healthcare, this similarity would be natural, as patients would be connected to others going through much the same pain and suffering. Timely and specific information, directed to the patient, could be made available to support groups, healthcare facilities, and healthcare providers. The technology exists to make this a reality and, with time, better-informed patients will be healthier and safer.

Power to the Individual

With information, interactivity and connectivity will come with a certain amount of power to the individual. In the past, people depended on a doctor and nurse for all needed medical procedures but going forward, this reliance will drastically decrease. Individuals will share in the responsibility for their own healthcare. They will become partners in healthcare, responsible for the health and well-being of the patient (self).

The same will be true of innovation creating a shared responsibility across departments, divisions, and organizations. The communication linkages will permit continuous sharing of information, project ideas, and future needs analysis. The collaboration of individuals in teams will be a natural state, even for virtual employees. With better communication and collaboration, needs will be better understood and addressed. This change will make for a more competitive environment and the need for innovation that much greater to distinguish the producer.

For healthcare, the natural accession of the individual and innovation projects needed for sustained success will greatly change the face and feel of the healthcare experience. Rather than often feeling like victims to an unresponsive and bloated bureaucracy, the individual will assume more responsibility while receiving the best healthcare available. It will be a paradigm-changing experience for all!

Summary

This chapter demonstrated the power of the individual in the innovation process. Discussed in this chapter was how the individual plays such a pivotal role in the initiation, transformation, and final success of innovation; in addition, how knowledge and personal experience affect the judgment of innovation and whether a change in behavior occurred. The individual controls the innovation process by both recognizing the innovation and taking action, or by not recognizing the event as innovative. This chapter explored current technologies and their ultimate effect on innovation in the future.

Discussion Questions

1. Describe your individual interests in innovation. How are these related to personal, professional, and organizational needs?
2. How would you evaluate the chances of innovation, in your healthcare organization or business, reaching the individual level?
3. Individuals submit their inventions ("new" innovations) for patent protection every day, yet so few make it to the marketplace. What are the reasons that many inventions never reach the general public?
4. Describe an innovation that someone (an individual) implemented in your organization or business. Was it something new, improved, or a change?

Assignments

1. Describe how you assess whether or not an item is innovative. Use Figure 10.1 as a place to start. Select an item that you recently purchased (or encountered) and thought was innovative. Do not forget to highlight the need (individual or corporate) that will be better satisfied.
2. Describe the approach you would implement to permit individuals to innovate freely within your business or healthcare facility. Consider elements such as
   a. Responsibilities and accountability
   b. Rewards and benefits
   c. Selection of individuals to innovate
   d. Support of leadership and management
   e. A simple process to evaluate needs (generated by customers, employees, suppliers, or stakeholders)

References

Adachi, W., and Lodolce, A. (2005) Use of failure mode and effects analysis in improving the safety of I.V. drug administration. *American Journal of Health-System Pharmacy,* 62(9), 917–920.

Agency for Health Research & Quality, Patient Safety Net (n.d.) Patient Safety Primers. Retrieved from http://psnet.ahrq.gov/ primer.aspx?primerID=3.

American Nurses Association (n.d.) Nursing-Sensitive Indicators. Retrieved from http://www.nursingworld.org/ MainMenuCategories/ThePracticeofProfessionalNursing/ PatientSafetyQuality/Research-Measurement/ The-National-Database/Nursing-Sensitive-Indicators_1.

Anonymous (2003) Idea experts roundtable. *The Futurist,* March/ April, p. 26–28.

Baregheh, A., Rowley, J., and Sambrook, S. (2009) Towards a multidisciplinary definition of innovation. *Management Decision,* 47(8), 1323–1339.

Barr, P. (2014) A Chronic Problem. Retrieved from http://www. hhnmag.com/display/HHN-news-article.dhtml?dcrPath=/ templatedata/HF_Common/NewsArticle/data/HHN/ Magazine/2014/Feb/fea-boomers-problems.

Bates, D.W., Kuperman, G.J., Wang, S., Gandhi, T., Kittler, A., Volk, L., Spurr, C., Khorasani, R., Tanasijevic, M., and Middleton, B. (2003) Ten Commandments for Effective Clinical Decision Support: Making the Practice of Evidence-Based Medicine a Reality. *J Am Med Inform Assoc,* Nov–Dec, 10(6), 523–530.

Baum, S. (2014a) Epic Veteran Sees an Opening in Developing Customized Apps for Providers. Retrieved from http:// medcitynews.com/2014/02/epic-veteran-sees-opening- developing-customized-apps-providers/#ixzz2u4NlGuUM.

Baum, S. (2014b) Can a Pre-operative Risk Assessment Tool Reduce Healthcare Costs and Improve Outcomes? Retrieved from http://medcitynews.com/2014/02/qpid-spinout-mass-general-rolls-pre-op-checklist/#ixzz2u4Z86aiY.

Bigliardi, B. (2013) The effect of innovation on financial performance: A research study involving SMEs. *Innovation: Management, Policy & Practice*, 15(2), 245–256. doi:10.5172/impp.2013.15.2.245.

Brasseur, C. (2013) Long-Term Outcomes Favor Heart Surgery over Stents and Angioplasty. Retrieved from http://www.sts.org/news/long-term-outcomes-favor-heart-surgery-over-stents-and-angioplasty.

Brown, B., and Anthony, S.D. (2011) How P&G tripled its innovation success rate. *Harvard Business Review,* 80(6), 63–72.

Caraballo, V., and McLaughlin, G. (2012). Individual perceptions of innovation: A multidimensional construct, *Journal of Business and Economics Research,* 10(10), 553–568.

Clark, C. (2014) Top Healthcare Quality Issues for 2014. Retrieved from http://www.healthleadersmedia.com/print/QUA-299700/Top-Healthcare-Quality-Issues-for-2014-Part-I.

CMS, Centers for Medicare & Medicaid Services (2007) State Medicaid Director Letter. Retrieved from http://downloads.cms.gov/cmsgov/archived-downloads/SMDL/downloads/SMD073108.pdf.

CMS, Centers for Medicare & Medicaid Services (2013) Final Policy and Payment Changes to the Medicare Physician Fee Schedule for Calendar Year 2014. Retrieved from http://www.cms.gov/Newsroom/MediaReleaseDatabase/Fact-Sheets/2013-Fact-Sheets-Items/2013-11-27-2.html?DLPage=1&DLSort=0&DLSortDir=descending.

CMS, Centers for Medicare & Medicaid Services. Innovation Center (n.d.) Innovation Models. Retrieved from http://innovation.cms.gov/initiatives/index.html.

CMS, Centers for Medicare & Medicaid Services (n.d.) Medicare Demonstration Projects & Evaluation Reports. Retrieved from http://www.cms.gov/Medicare/Demonstration-Projects/DemoProjectsEvalRpts/Medicare-Demonstrations.html.

Claridge, J.A., and Fabian, T.C. (2005) History and development of evidence based medicine. *World Journal of Surgery*, p. 548. Doi 101007/s00268-005-7910-1.

Clark, C. (2014) Top Healthcare Quality Issues for 2014. Retrieved from http://www.healthleadersmedia.com/print/QUA-299700/Top-Healthcare-Quality-Issues-for-2014-Part-I.

Combes, J. (2014) Physician Leaders in a Transformed System. Retrieved from http://www.hhnmag.com/display/HHN-news-article.dhtml?dcrPath=/templatedata/HF_Common/NewsArticle/data/HHN/Magazine/2014/Feb/aha-voices-physician-leadership&utm_source=daily&utm_medium=email&utm_campaign=%20HHN.

Crane, J., and Noon, C.E. (2011) *The Definitive Guide to Emergency Department Operational Improvement: Employing Lean Principles with Current ED Best Practices to Create the "No Wait" Department*. Taylor & Francis Group, Boca Raton, FL.

Dahl, A, Lawrence, J., and Pierce, J. (2011) Building an innovation community. *Research–Technology Management*, September-October, p. 19–27.

Dartmouth Atlas of Health Care. (2010) http://www.dartmouthatlas.org

Davies, G., Chun, R., Kamins, M. (2010) Reputation gaps and the performance of service organizations. *Strategic Management Journal*, 31(5), 463–574.

Deloitte (2012) A View of the US Health Care System. Retrieved from https://www.deloitte.com/view/en_US/us/Industries/US-federal-government/center-for-health-solutions/c36a21fb2d2e8310VgnVCM3000001c56f00aRCRD.htm.

de Waal, A., Maritz, A., and Shieh, C. (2010) Managing innovation: A typology of theories and practiced-based implications for New Zealand firms. *International Journal of Organizational Innovation*, 3(2), 35–57.

Dougwood (2014, January 15). Re: Future of Healthcare [Web log comment]. Retrieved from http://futureofhealthcareblog.mayoclinic.org/discussion/the-center-for-innovation-shaping-the-future-of-health-care.

Eccles, R.G., and Serafeim, G. (2013) The performance frontier. *Harvard Business Review*, 91(5), 50–60.

Evans, M. (2014) Healthcare Job Losses in January Signal that Hiring Slowdown Continues. Retrieved from http://www.modernhealthcare.com/article/20140208/MAGAZINE/302089978/healthcare-job-losses-in-january-signal-that-hiring-slowdown.

Fleuren, M., Wiefferink, K., and Paulussen, T. (2004) Determinants of innovation with healthcare organizations. *Int J Qual Health Care,* 16(2): 107-123. doi: 10.1093/intqhc/mzh030

Friedman, E. (2014) Stopping Dr. Feelgood: The Challenge of Overprescribing. Retrieved from http://www.hhnmag.com/display/HHN-news-article.dhtml?dcrPath=/template-data/HF_Common/NewsArticle/data/HHN/Daily/2014/Feb/020414-article-Emily-Friedman-precription-drugs&utm_source=Daily&utm_medium=email&utm_campaign=general.

Gawande, A. (2009) *The Checklist Manifesto.* Metropolitan Books. Henry Holt and Company, New York.

Gold, J. (2014) How Parents and the Internet Transformed Clubfoot Treatment. Retrieved from http://www.npr.org/blogs/health/2014/01/27/265254533/how-parents-and-the-internet-transformed-clubfoot-treatment.

Group Health (2014) The Chronic Care Model. Retrieved from http://www.improvingchroniccare.org/index.php?p=the_chronic_care_model&s=2

Hamer, S., Plochg, T., and Moreira, P. (2012) Healthcare innovation. *International Journal of Healthcare Management*, 5(4), 187.

Harrop-Griffiths, W. (2011) Never events. *Anaesthesia*, 66(3), 158–162. doi:10.1111/j.1365-2044.2010.06624.x.

Heckley, P. (2014) Paul Heckley on 2014 Health Care Trends. Retrieved from http://www.hhnmag.com/display/HHN-news-article.dhtml?dcrPath =/te…4-outlook&utm_source=Daily&utm_medium=email&utm_campaign=general.

HHS. (2002) US Department of Health & Human Services. http://www.hhs.gov/asl/testify/t020523a.html

HIMSS (Health Information Management Systems Society) (2014) Mobile Technology Survey. http://www.himssanalytics.org/research/AssetDetail.aspx?pubid=81559&tid=131.

Houle, S., McAlister, F., Jackevicius, C., Chuck, A., and Tsuyuki, R. (2012). Does performance-based remuneration for individual health care practitioners affect patient care?: A systematic review. *Annals of Internal Medicine*, 157(12), 889–899. doi:10.7326/0003-4819-157-12-201212180-00009.

Hull, C., and Rothenberg, S. (2008). Firm performance: The inter-actions of corporate social performance with innovation and industry differentiation. *Strategic Management Journal*, 29(7), 781–789.

Industry Browser—Yahoo Finance (2014). Retrieved from http://biz.yahoo.com/p/5conameu.html.

Institute for Healthcare Improvement (2004) Retrieved from http://jdc.jefferson.edu/cgi/viewcontent.cgi?article=1470&context=hpn&sei-redir=1&referer=http%3A%2F%2Fscholar.google.com%2Fscholar%3Fq=5000+lives+and+berwick%26btnG=%26hl=en%26as_sdt=0,45-search="5000livesberwick".

Institute for Healthcare Improvement (ihi.org) (2014) SBAR: Situation-Background-Assessment-Recommendation. http://www.ihi.org/Topics/SBARCommunicationTechnique/Pages/default.aspx

IOM, Institute of Medicine (1999) Crossing the Quality Chasm. Retrieved from http://www.iom.edu/~/media/Files/Report%20Files/2001/Crossing-the-Quality-Chasm/Quality%20Chasm%202001%20%20report%20brief.pdf.

IOM, Institute of Medicine (2001) Crossing the Quality Chasm. A New Health System for the 21st Century. Retrieved from http://www.iom.edu/Reports/2001/Crossing-the-Quality-Chasm-A-New-Health-System-for-the-21st-Century.aspx.

IOM, Institute of Medicine (2010) The Future of Nursing. Retrieved from http://www.iom.edu/reports/2010/the-future-of-nursing-leading-change-advancing-health.aspx.

Intermountain Healthcare (n.d.) Institute for Healthcare Delivery Research. Retrieved from http://intermountainhealthcare.org/qualityandresearch/institute/alumniresources/Pages/home.aspx

Jana, R. (2007) A chorus of voices is calling for an end to the hype—and a focus on what really drives profitable innovation. *Businessweek*, (4025), 28.

Johnson, S.R. (2014) Getting to the Root of the Problem. Retrieved from http://www.modernhealthcare.com/article/20140201/MAGAZINE/302019986/getting-to-the-root-of-the-problem.

Kaiser Permanente (n.d.) ALL/Phase. Retrieved from http://share.kaiserpermanente.org/article/safety-net-partnerships-quality-improvement-and-population-health/#sthash.PT2Q9gV7.dpuf.

Kim, J. (2013) Automated Diagnostics: How Supercomputers Fit in Radiology's Future. Retrieved from http://searchhealthit.techtarget.com/feature/Automated-diagnostics-How-

supercomputers-fit-in-radiologys-future?src=5215000&asrc=EM_
ERU_26749261&uid=16343684&utm_medium=EM&utm_
source=ERU&utm_campaign=20140224_ERU+Transmission+for
+02%2F24%2F2014+%28UserUniverse%3A+681996%29_myka-
reports%40techtarget.com.

Leapfrog Group (2013) Hidden Surcharge Calculator. Retrieved from
http://www.leapfroggroup.org/HiddenSurchargeCalculator.

Lee, J. (2014) Selling Doctors, Not Hospitals. Retrieved from
http://www.modernhealthcare.com/article/20131019/
MAGAZINE/310199974/selling-hospitals-not-doctors.

Liu, H., Moynihan, K.D., Zheng, Y., Szeto, G.L., Li, A.V., Huang, B.,
Van Egernen, D.S., Park, C., and Irvine, D.J. (2014) Structure-
based programming of lymph-node targeting in molecular
vaccines. doi:10.1038/nature12978. Retrieved from http://www.
nature.com/nature/journal/vaop/ncurrent/full/nature12978.html

Mace, S. (2104) In search of EHR's ROI. *Healthcare Leaders,* 17(1), 12.

Mace, S. (2013) How Population Health Analytics Opens
Opportunities for Better Care. Retrieved from http://www.
healthleadersmedia.com/content/TEC-298525/How-Population-
Health-Analytics-Opens-Opportunities-for-Better-Care.html##.

Marshall, L., Hagood, C., Royer, A., Reece, C.P., and Maloney, S.
(2006). Using Lean methods to improve OR turnover times.
Association of Operating Room Nurses.AORN Journal, 84(5),
849–855. doi:http://dx.doi.org/10.1016/S0001-2092(06)63971-9.

McKinney, M. (2014) Hospitals Simple Intervention Reduce Alarm
Fatigue. Retrieved from http://www.modernhealthcare.com/
article/20140201/MAGAZINE/30201996.

McLaughlin, G. (1995) *Total Quality In Research and Development,*
St. Lucie Press, Delray Beach, FL, p. 96.

McLaughlin, G. (2012, June 25) Why innovation is so often hit or
miss, *Innovation Management,* retrieved from http://www.
innovationmanagement.se/.

McLaughlin, G., and V. Caraballo (2013a) *Chance or Choice:
Unlocking Innovation Success,* Taylor & Francis Group, Boca
Raton, FL.

McLaughlin, G., and V. Caraballo (2013b) *ENOVALE: How to Unlock
Sustained Innovation Project Success,* Taylor & Francis Group,
Boca Raton, FL.

McNichol, E. (2012) Patient-led innovation in healthcare: The value
of the 'user' perspective. *Journal of Healthcare Management,*
5(4), 216–222.

Millard, M. (2103) Big Growth Seen for Device Integration. Retrieved from http://www.healthcareitnews.com/news/big-growth-seen-device-integration.

Molpus, J. (2013) Uncovering cost savings. *Health Leaders*, 1(16), 60–62.

Monegain, B. (2014) Deloitte Taps the Zen of Analytics. Retrieved from http://www.healthcareitnews.com/news/deloitte-taps-zen-data-analytics?topic=02,06,19.

Paladino, A. (2009). Financial champions and masters of Innovation: Analyzing the effects of balancing strategic orientations. *Journal of Product Innovation Management*, 26(6), 616-626. doi:10.1111/j.1540-5885.2009.00687.

Pogoric, D. (2014) Diabetics + Patient Navigators Improved Blood Glucose Control by 32% in Cleveland Clinic Pilot. Retrieved from http://medcitynews.com/2014/02/patient-navigators-helped-diabetics-improve-blood-glucose-control-32-cleveland-clinic-pilot/#ixzz2tcn0JoAV.

Porter O'Grady, T. (2014) From tradition to transformation: A revolutionary moment for nursing in the age of reform. *Nurse Leader*, 1(12), 59–65.

Pub-Med (2012) The Basic Principles of Evidence Based Medicine. Retrieved from http://www.ncbi.nlm.nih.gov/pubmedhealth/PMH0005078/.

Pub-Med (2013) About Clinical Effectiveness Research. Retrieved from http://www.ncbi.nlm.nih.gov/pubmedhealth/aboutcer/.

Rau, A. (2014) Integrating Yoga into Medical Practice—It's More Than 'Just Relaxation Response. Retrieved from http://capsules.kaiserhealthnews.org/index.php/2014/02/integrating-yoga-into-medical-practice-its-more-than-just-relaxation-response/#more-26166.

Rau, J. (2103) 1,450 Hospitals Penalized by Medicare. Retrieved from http://www.healthcarefinancenews.com/news/1450-hospitals-penalized-medicare.

Robeznieks, A. (2014) Prospering by Standardizing Processes and Improving the Patient Experience. Retrieved from http://www.modernhealthcare.com/article/20140111/MAGAZINE/301119950/prospering-by-standardizing-processes-and-improving-the-patient.

Robinson, C., and Goudy, K. (2009) Leadership in these challenging times. *Frontiers of Health Services Management*, 26(2), 21–26.

Rotherman-Borus, M., Swendeman, D., and Chorpita, B. (2012). Disruptive innovations for designing and diffusing evidence-based interventions. *American Psychologist,* 67(6), 463–476.

Sharma, V. (2013) Earned value management: A tool for project performance. *Advances in Management,* 6(5), 37–42.

Shulman, R.S. (2006) Material whirl. *Marketing Management,* 15(2), 25–27.

Stewart, C., Hurst, D., Worden, C. and Rabinovitch, R. (2013) Less is better: A creative approach to decreasing healthcare-associated surgical site infections using a modified root cause analysis. *American Journal of Infection Control,* 39(5), 146.

The Joint Commission (2013) The Joint Commission History (2013) Retrieved from http://www.jointcommission.org/assets/1/6/Joint_Commission_History.pdf

The Joint Commission (2013) ORYX Project. Retrieved from http://www.jointcommission.org/search/default.aspx?Keywords=oryx&f=sitename&sitename=Joint+Commission.

The Joint Commission (2013) Root Cause Analysis. Retrieved from http://www.jointcommission.org/Framework_for_Conducting_a_Root_Cause_Analysis_and_Action_Plan/

The Joint Commission (n.d.) Standards. http://www.jointcommission.org/standards_information/tjc_requirements.aspx

Thomke, S. (2002) *Innovation at 3M Corporation.* Cambridge, MA: Harvard Business School Press.

Turner, R., and Zolin, R. (2012) Forecasting success on large projects: Developing reliable scales to predict multiple perspectives by multiple stakeholders over multiple time frames. *Project Management Journal,* 43(5), 83–89.

Van Wijngaarden, J., Botje, D., Illianc, S., van der Waa, N., Mendes, R., Hamerm, S., and Plochg, T. (2012) How doctor involvement in management affects innovation. *International Journal of Healthcare Management,* 5(4), 203–207.

Virginia Mason Production System (n.d.) Retrieved from https://www.virginiamason.org/vmps.

Wayne, A. (2012, June 12) Healthcare Spending to Rise to 20% of U.S. Economy by 2012. Bloomberg Politics. Retrieved from http://www.bloomberg.com/news/2012-06-13/health-care-spending-to-reach-20-of-u-s-economy-by-2021.html.

Wicklund, E. (2013) FDA Gets Thumbs Up on Mobile Apps Regs. Retrieved from http://www.healthcareitnews.com/news/fda-gets-thumbs-mobile-apps-regs.

Wood, D.L. (2014) The Center for Innovation Shaping the Future of Health Care. Retrieved from http://futureofhealthcareblog.mayoclinic.org/discussion/the-center-for-innovation-shaping-the-future-of-health-care.

Wyden, R. (2014) The Better Care, Lower Cost Act of 2014. Retrieved from http://www.wyden.senate.gov/download/bill-text_the-better-care-lower-cost-act-of-2014.

Zeis, M. (2013) Medicine based on knowledge. *Health Leaders*, 16(1), 27–29.

Zhuang, L. (1995) Bridging the gap between technology and business strategy: A pilot study on the innovation process. *Management Decision*, 33(8), 13–19.

Zhuang, L., Williamson, D., and Carter, M. (1999) Innovate or liquidate: Are all organizations convinced? A two-phased study into the innovation process. *Management Decisions*, 37(1), 57–71.

Index

Note: Page numbers ending in "f" refer to figures. Page numbers ending in "t" refer to tables.

219

ENOVALE process. *See also*
  ENOVALE Solutions;
  ENOVALE Strategies
  adaptation stage, 80, 101
  alignment stage, 80, 102–105
  analysis stage, 102–105
  cause-and-effect matrix, 102,
    103f
  Control FMEA tool, 106–107, 107f
  elements of, 180t–181t
  evolving concept, 77–78
  execution stage, 82–83, 106–108
  explanation of, 17–18, 31–33
  FMEA tool, 102, 104f, 106–107,
    107f
  identifying opportunities, 98–99
  for improvements, 97–98
  for innovation, 31–33, 32f, 91–106
  for leadership, 179–185, 180t–181t
  model for, 31–33, 32f
  negotiation stage, 78–79
  "new" items, 77–78, 77f
  "new" project theme, 81–82, 82f
  objective of, 77–83
  operational profile, 101–102
  originality levels, 69, 79
  overperformance and, 98–101
  performance links, 81–82, 82f,
    105–106, 106f
  for project success, 72–84
  SMPA diagram, 99–101, 100f
  steps in, 77–83, 77f, 82f
  strategies of, 83, 91f, 94, 97–108,
    114–129
  "test of reality" for, 78–79
  underperformance and,
    101–108
  validation stage, 99, 101, 102
  verification stage, 80
ENOVALE Solutions
  for change, 115–116
  for high-level management,
    30–31, 30f

for improvement project, 91–92,
    91f, 94–95
  for intangible items, 93–94
  for project success, 72–77, 77f,
    133–134, 139
  for tangible items, 92–93
ENOVALE Strategies, 83, 91f, 94,
    97–108, 112f, 115–120
Ethical principles, 118, 169, 184, 186
Ethnic issues, 14, 34, 198–199
Evidence-based initiatives (EBIs), 3,
    7–8, 37

F

Failure
  consequences of, 24, 34, 116–117
  cost of, 30
  identifying, 102, 106–108, 110,
    116
  indicators for, 34–35
  learning from, 146, 172–173, 184
  reasons for, 71–72, 71f, 113, 146
  reducing, 97–98, 129–130
  responsibility for, 164, 169,
    172–173, 184
  risk and, 118–121, 129–130
Failure modes and effectiveness
    analysis (FMEA), 12–13, 102,
    104f, 106–107, 107f
Fee-for-service, 23, 26, 149–150
Financial measures, 131–132,
    135–136, 146
For-profit organizations, 132,
    135–136, 198
Future innovation
  aging populations, 147, 160–162,
    164
  alternative medicine, 162–163
  analytics for, 153–155
  electronic medical records,
    152–154
  implications for, 150–159